T0117331

KD

Selected Works by Dave Oliphant:

Poetry

Brands
Taking Stock
Lines & Mounds
Austin
Maria's Poems
Memories of Texas Towns & Cities
Backtracking

Memoir

Harbingers of Books to Come: A Texan's Literary Life

Criticism & History

On a High Horse: Views Mostly of Latin American & Texan Poetry
Texan Jazz
The Early Swing Era, 1930 to 1941
Jazz Mavericks of the Lone Star State

Edited

Contemporary Chilean Poetry
The New Breed: An Anthology of Texas Poets
Washing the Cow's Skull / Lavando la Calavera de Vaca
Roundup: An Anthology of Texas Poets

Translated

If Poetry Is To Be Written Right, by Enrique Lihn
Figures of Speech, by Enrique Lihn
Love Hound, by Oliver Welden
After-Dinner Declarations, by Nicanor Parra

KD

a *Jazz* Biography

by Dave Oliphant

WingsPress

San Antonio, Texas
2012

Print Edition ISBN: 978-0-916727-95-6
ePub ISBN: 978-1-60940-213-6
Kindle ISBN: 978-1-60940-214-3
Library PDF ISBN: 978-1-60940-215-0

Wings Press
627 E. Guenther
San Antonio, Texas 78210
Phone/fax: (210) 271-7805

On-line catalogue and ordering:
www.wingspress.com
All Wings Press titles are distributed to the trade by
Independent Publishers Group
www.ipgbook.com

Library of Congress Cataloging-in-Publication Data:

Oliphant, Dave.
KD : a jazz biography / by Dave Oliphant.
p. cm.
ISBN 978-0-916727-95-6 (hardback, printed edition : alk. paper) -- ISBN 978-1-60940-213-6 (epub ebook) -- ISBN 978-1-60940-214-3 (kindle ebook) -- ISBN 978-1-60940-215-0 (library pdf ebook)
1. Dorham, Kenny, 1924-1972. 2. Jazz musicians--United States--Biography. 3. Trumpet players--United States--Biography. I. Title.
ML419.D68O45 2012
788.9'2165092--dc23
[B]

2011045237

Contents

KD

Viking in Reverse

did biblical Ham ever come near
in the prince's mind a prison cell
but for the Texas bop trumpeteer
Denmark meant was treated well

from live tapings in Copenhagen
at the Montmartre Jazzhus in '63
hear *Short Story* KD's hardy CD
bears his name in black on green

its title tune taken Sheridan says
in part from "Tickletoe" by Prez
or a "head" remembered by Ken
& his four all-European sidemen

but doesn't include Rolf Ericson
whose trumpet *is* on another CD
from this land of a midnight sun
KD's *Scandia Skies* it too from '63

December 5th his other from 19th
with title tune to render tribute to
being in cold so warmly received
by that city & by its music venue

"It Could Happen to You" a hall-
mark solo by each then RE alone
on Bonfá's "Manhã de Carnaval"
its bossa nova Ken'd heard in '61

& on *Short Story* that same piece
but there it's a southwestern tone
with K probing at his loping pace
& "São Paulo" K's entitled home

of prodigious João Carlos Martins
pianist who recorded all of Bach's
preludes gigues fugues & gavottes
corrente notes as if fins in streams

just as Kenny too can fish-like zig
zag leap & flash & the current dig
but couldn't have caught him live
yet Brazil in *Una más* reissue '95

floats there on Lerner & Loewe's
"If Ever I Would Leave You" o's
slowed until they're "bittersweet"
then subtly trills to its bossa beat

by the '90s Arthur Moreira Lima
reviving Ernesto Nazareth in Rio
he whose "Travesso" can seem a
Joplin rag more so Chopin tango

recalls in '94 on her wedding day
Elisa's paying for Russell to play
to lilt EN's "Confidências" at Inn
on the Creek to where was driven

by Milo dreamed-of carriage ride
from chapel to reception as bride
to her Brazilian groom their cake
shared decades after KD to make

his Danish dates unheard till '93
on Nils Winther's SteepleChase
the Bird's tune he chose to base
his label on in Parker's memory

his forebears who had never cut
nor mixed a disc but adzed long
serpented ships flexible enough
to take the waves & never bang

smooth & sleek as they cleaved
a sea & K notes sailed the same
through his lanky Texian frame
his melodiousness light beneath

an overcast sky as Scandinavian
as Rolf's last & illustrious name
through it perhaps Rolf even kin
to the one named new lands Vin

Leif the Lucky discoverer from
the end of that first millennium
on bass it's the prodigy at just 17
Niels-Henning Ørsted Pedersen

whose line's more likely related
to the marauders of monasteries
to Kiev founders told the stories
of Sigurd Fafnirsbane was fated

to slay a dragon drink her blood
& from it draw the secret words
uttered in conversing with birds
whose sense but she understood

a mocker Kenny's sort of singer
whose tones rarely if ever linger
its rhythms & refrains inventive
hardly repeating so imaginative

unstuck on a monotonous pitch
a bobwhite's two-toned whistle
or the grackle's ignition switch
K & the mocker more variable

the CD insert photo a close-up
of his dark pin-striped suit hair
& skin contrasting with a glare
from white shirt-collar & cuffs

his valve caps under fingertips
his horn's mouthpiece pressed
against the all-but-unseen lips
head tilted down toward Alex

Riel's upward slanted cymbal
forming a sort of halo behind
Kenny's slightly angled hand
as third finger pushes middle

valve halfway down for mel-
ancholy with tongue aflutter
flatting a 5th in a major scale
for blue minor never despair

but how here in frozen fjords
if on a Brazos farm scorched
by mid July what skaldic age
knew that southwest passage

not even metaphysical Donne
yet K would find & take com-
fort in Spain's Tete Montoliu
in the Allan Botschinsky flue-

gelhorn & in his mix of Danes
& Swedes & with Norwegians
January '64 at Oslo Metropole
issued on '92 Landscape label

but there his descent different
from Miles's on J.J. "Lament"
K pouring down as a waterfall
cataracting into unfathomable

depths ascending to intensities
buoyed by rippling liquid keys
as Tore Sannes softly tremolos
to heighten KD's soaring solos

another Pedersen on bass Björn
his given name & a Christensen
Jon joining on drums to explore
that heart of darkness continent

with this seer of northern lights
who had ancestors been unsold
unshipped in a perdition's hold
chanting tribal rhythmical rites

unground by subjugation's mill
not tilled their New World field
had never known blues' mystery
had never failed in his chemistry

his physics either or on the road
come to hear with Isaac Newton
ears an equal & counter reaction
rocket's red flare blast & payload

taking lessons as if from Viking 8
or any flight with all of its weight
a strewn wreckage if its fiery hull
unlifting from a gravitational pull

though Ken would learn it through
a Poppa Dip who had broken loose
Bohr too with his quantum theories
hydrogen lines in a spectrum series

with light emitted inside his reactor
as its slow neutron or divided atom
leaped away at angular momentum
Niels depicts in a kitchen metaphor

of the simple tap with its water drip
its fission as in a trumpeter's falling
from his long glissando to split a lip
Bohr's earlier work Einstein calling

a kind of music of the highest form
father of A bomb but first to charm
all those within his realm of thought
to sail for Baltic ports & if K caught

a plane instead not for any theorem
but proof of an energy in every beat
for if in physics Ken never received
any passing grade was still to blend

a science of sound with an alchemy
for radiating electrical orbital notes
Niels' own at risk from Nazi shoats
both wavelength & starred ancestry

but aided by those crafty Norsemen
whose descendants too abetted Ken
their intrepid sagas lettered as runes
the Greek & Latin etched on stones

riveting planks for the rugged firth
floated as K would from bar to bar
each fashioned by a Post Oak birth
by Austin & Marshall prior to war

later tempered in Oakland & NYC
put through bop's exams by Dizzy
& Bird & by Fats' red freezing ice
by Eckstine's band & later Horace

Art & KD first Messengers to deliv-
er the word & then in '56 Ken with
his Prophets spreading it too as J.R.
Monterose on tenor'd peck in order

now here composes for blonde blue-
eyed scions of rovers' coastal pillage
Thor obeyed on whale road & slough
though KD's trip required no portage

no dragging of keels nor a battle gear
no barter goods hauled from Dnieper
down to Byzantium rather his arrival
come by a separate & unequal school

where they jeered at a blow-boy sissy
where at recess its playground's bully
in wait for dishing out a daily socking
& in self-defense he'd take up boxing

& on receiving Draft Board greetings
sparred a bit but handed best beatings
by Gillespie pugilistic big-band brass
punched it out taking licks seated last

holding his own with a Navarro & Stitt
in separate late-summer sessions of'46
yet wasn't to go the full bruising round
as did in Dallas both Handy & Garland

in a then smoke-filled Deep Ellum ring
duked it out for ten neither taking dives
later to lay down chords but in winning
at the bell just belted by Golden Gloves

lacing them on with their knuckles sore
then hung them up for those studio gigs
for the solos after they'd signed up with
Miles or Mingus & then a battling more

with a needle's allure the deeper release
promise of nuanced tone a locked-hands
sonic boom Kenny too to know its tease
but his a higher flying over Greenland's

arctic arm & the island Danes possessed
their Faroe & as well Brahe's Uraniborg
where for science's sake he'd impressed
his peasants for the constellation formed

above K's boyhood home later he'd fear
going up on stage with a Diz or Brownie
the Extra headline shouted for all to hear
"Superstar Fades KD a Fallen Luminary"

but not giving up K simply never would
from his lungs to every lymphatic gland
would dedicate all to give & take could
count him in & on him to play his hand

just passing then over Kronborg Castle
by way of Elsinore & a sound-toll fund
Tyco collected for erecting his celestial
globe to track the galaxies gyre around

& then to predict the next conjunction
of Mars with the Moon in Orion's foot
could fix the comet's parallax position
Hven's findings sent from his Institute

as through his press he published word
of stellar harmony as on any LP record
KD made but aligning no special view
nothing in his cosmos so Yardbird new

offered no supernovas leaping forward
to swing on axis of his musical spheres
never claimed as Tyco did to be a Lord
of any skies K no egocentric as appears

in Ty's Urania elegy & its praise of will
conceives the soul as an unforced mind
declaring but a few can manage to bend
the stars to their own rule could in exile

& yet though Ty notating sightings right
Kepler would find all his ellipses wrong
could it ever apply in the world of song
a Ptolemy out of tune in a Tunisia night

if Ken toured Ty's mural & his azimuth
saw quadrants ponds & fountain sluices
caught their geometrical design or from
hidden tubes the concordant microcosm

he may have flipped but on "Our Thing"
did K in '63 half think or intend to bring
seasonal winds together the hot cold wet
& dry to form some black hipper Hamlet

or ever see himself as Beowulf taking on
a Grendel in a test of bare-fisted strength
famed branded banned moors-fen demon
whose blood thirst a thane had quenched

or consider turning into Heorot's savior
quaffing honey meads with a ring-giver
or KOing as Brown Bomber had in '38
the Führer's own pure super Aryan race

or outrun the field as did a Jesse Owens
threw in Hitler's plan a monkey wrench
when with four golds sprinter would nix
Adolf's grand '36 propaganda Olympics

or decry in ten acts as did from his pulpit
a Kaj Munk that clergyman & playwright
who braved Herod's iron-cross swastikas
till they'd drag his corpse through ditches

rather than those K & Co. arranged a head
rendered as their soulful hard-bop version
of Lester's '40 riff on Basie's famous side
with tenor Buddy Tate KD's fellow Texan

waxed the same year fabled Valaida Snow
the Chattanooga singer & Trumpet Queen
had been she would say interned by Dan-
ish police thank goodness not by Gestapo

on July 26 recorded her "St. Louis Blues"
with their local band of Winstrup Olesen
black star decked out in a pale orchid suit
dazzled with her vocal jive & biting tone

reminding now of Prez's '45 "DB Blues"
titled on being stationed & remanded to
the detention barracks on facing another
trumped up charge of a Jim Crow major

in digging around to find in a footlocker
Prez's white wife's photograph to main-
tain his pills illegal those the G.I. doctor
prescribed for severe rectal surgery pain

Val detained in a Danish camp up to '42
kept away from decadent Scandinavians
thrived on jazz even the SS sneaked it in
Danes crossing over to Skåne 7000 Jews

would save David stars by private boats
& in '39 gave welcome to jazz's royalty
the Duke & his orchestra's indigo notes
still reigning in ears with love & loyalty

& the leader & his men knew them true
for on "Jack the Bear" the Blanton bass
remains inspired propelled by the place
"Serenade to Sweden" pays homage to

with Ellington at his piano so subdued
it makes it so trumpeter Wallace Jones
must whisper softly with flowery mute
to Lawrence Brown's subtle trombone

then Carney on his nonpareil baritone
reaches into the reed's supernal range
to anchor & preserve those drift alone
on emotion's waves wreck or estrange

in '50 Bird would arrive in Stockholm
to a Bromma airport crowd so welcom-
ing it astonished him while he for Lars
Werner *the* experience of all his years

forever moved by the concert & a jam
session later at Helsingborg when sax-
ophonist improvised with a deep relax-
ing feel on "Star Eyes" & too on "Em-

braceable You" though "Body & Soul"
not up to that amazing rendition of '42
in part from the drummer's over intru-
sive kit or perhaps with Parker too full

of Swedish schnapps not yet that tune
would record with Red Rodney in '51
but that gin drink he gave it as its title
after the visit to Lars so unforgettable

as it must've been for any who heard
& were touched by the genius of Bird
& surely again in '53 when a Clifford
Brown'd arrive in their land to record

with Swedish All-Stars Quincy Jones'
"Stockholm Sweetnin'" would amaze
as well with a trumpet sound & phras-
ing rich in stimulating luxurious tones

& even before his chorus a reliable Art
Farmer no slouch at all shared the solo
space with his own fine showing smart
unflamboyant a morsel tasty & mellow

& again in '61 Lars with Bertil Sundin
asserting Monk in Stockholm had been
among their very greatest moments yet
album out of print only burnt duplicate

Lon Armstrong made attests to an *Or-
kester Journalen* review wherein Bertil
wrote of the High Priest-Rouse perfor-
mance "swung so could hardly sit still"

in "I'm Getting Sentimental Over You"
the pianist's dramatic timing's unerring
as ever the scalar runs surprising anew
tenor's infectious if not ever so stirring

in '58 the Dave Brubeck Quartet came
to delight the Danes on doing that tune
from Danny Kaye's movie made in '52
based on Anderson of a fairy tale fame

hear now the audience clapping in time
to their own "Wonderful Copenhagen"
with Paul Desmond's dancing alto ring
while Dave's waltzing its happy theme

in '59 the Gillespie Quintet in concert
showcasing Leo Wright's alto & flute
his lightning runs & his thunder burst
one other fellow Texan so overlooked

in '60 an MJQ "Django" in Göteborg
with its majestic Jackson mallet work
celebrating burnt-fingered Reinhardt
rang with two digits his gypsy guitar

Heath's ostinato bass pumps it out
& Kay's always tasteful cymbal fills
press till Lewis' piano gingerly builds
to his blues-striding whispered shout

as members of their sound ensemble
making music from the heart & soul
each recognized by his touch & tone
on the instrument he's made his own

in following year Basie with a palm
for joy spread to Swedish hinterland
towns Varnamo Borgholm on Öland
isle & Malmö before the Stockholm

concerts at Gröna Lunds where Ake
Persson sat in on "Blues Backstage"
& the Swede took a gutbucket page
out of Ory for a hip trombone break

& Texan Henry Coker answered on
an arrangement of "In a Mellotone"
with his stylish 'bone & on trumpet
Fip Ricard a ball in "Corner Pocket"

in '61 too Eric Dolphy with Danes
Erik Moseholm on bass Bent Axen
keyboard & Jorn Elniff percussion
jam-packing Studenterforeningens

the Copenhagen lecture hall where
after "The Way You Look Tonight"
after Eric's bop tags so out of sight
unison applause calls for an encore

then renders "Laura" with allusion
to "Pop Goes the Weasel" not only
proves the relativity of either's key
but a free jazz meaning serious fun

from lands old & new light or dark
old-time hits fit for the avant-garde
quotation of Mother Goose rhymes
an Ornette Tchaikovsky lick in '59

after it in '65 to rouse a Stockholm
with his raucous alto right at home
to let "Snowflakes & Sunshine" in
on his self-taught trumpet & violin

for "Riddle" & "Antiques" joined
by David Izenzon's classical bass
Charles Moffett's drums roof-rais-
ing or bell soft on "Morning Song"

a sequencing termed "pure beauty"
his optimism not alone the Swede
receives at its Golden Circle duty
free but filling every crying need

then for '64 Albert Ayler Quartet
with pixy Cherry pocket trumpet
turning on on *Copenhagen Tapes*
following in Coleman's footsteps

in his boyish voice Albert himself
recalls in high school oboe & golf
says in Scandinavia feels truly free
one day U.S. to be as it ought to be

"Children" with its whines & yells
pitches the typical temper tantrum
"Mothers" outlandish romanticism
"Saints" quote recalls the spirituals

"Vibrations" fitting of crisis to a T
as Gary plucks & on drums Sunny
wails converting pop Swedish folk-
songs to their "Spirits" & "Ghosts"

no language Kenny spoke but who
knows he could have learned it too
& yet neither outrage nor exorcism
his shtick his a calid holistic tongue

as the Hans "Hornbook" alphabet's
open to both sides secular & sacred
closes the generational gap with its
troop of signs will rout white or red

upon the letter order written or said
so much depends either glad or sad
with D in Denmark his bonnie land
God shield it in his protective hand

C for Columbus at Amerigo's shore
turning a world twice its size before
while KD's book just flats & sharps
no verbal notes & no nautical charts

yet K's to out sail even Christopher
since along with travel transatlantic
he'll cover seas the Admiral missed
on his "Bombay" & "Lotus Flower"

& if K's Half Note "Jong Fu" of '66
came in wake of such oriental motifs
as Fletcher Henderson's '24 "Shang-
hai Shuffle" Ben Pollack '28 "Sing-

apore Sorrows" & in between Louie
with a killer '26 "Cornet Chop Suey"
in '31 "China Boy" of Fats & Big T
& in '40 Cab's "Chop Chop Charlie

Chan" yet still K'd map in "Mexico
City" "Tahitian Suite" "São Paulo"
& "Monaco" cosmographies Brahe
with all his scopes would never see

& if K borrowed had not a Brahms
& for sound tracks to western films
most out of Copland's *Billy the Kid*
on which changes has jazz not lived

with “Prince Albert” he would seize
the day from Kern’s rich harmonies
in “All the Things You Are” & then
partly to pattern “DX” on Gershwin

“I Got Rhythm” taken in every way
& “Don’t Explain” a Billie Holiday
U for Uppsala that’s a stately town
find on the globe its name set down

northwest of “Dear Old Stockholm”
where its folk tune Getz would hear
or must assume since cannot phone
to ask Meehan so admired his tenor

the Davis ’56 Quintet cut it for sure
with Red feeding ’Trane the chords
for his o there aren’t enough words
not even Hans’ can hope to capture

though maybe in “Golden Treasure”
where his drummer boy is off to war
the father’s proud the mother fearful
both the tale & explication an earful

but lacks the All-American Rhythm
that section of Paul Chambers’ bass
Philly Joe’s sticks & Garland states
with elegance Miles’ Scandia theme

after Satchelmouth had set the pace
with a ’24 solo on Henderson’s side
of a tune of Indiana’s Charlie Davis
so curious how he’d come to decide

on "Copenhagen" a title's abstruse
mysterious in origin unlike a blues
or the Savannah-born "Yamekraw"
of James P. Johnson striding Paw

Dipper's maybe is more complex
than the one of Wolverines & Bix
whose dah-dotdotdot of May 26th
to reverse no victory of Ludwig's

nor to send a message of distress
theirs a reply to fog-bound ships
& if Morse's code is now retired
such a short-long sound inspired

the Mahler *Fifth* can ever rescue
by its rhythmic numerical magic
in that 4-note trumpet call or too
any blown by Bunk Beiderbecke

or Ken with his counter-reacting
style of running like Jesse's stole
the show & if KD'd won no poll
to Blakey still the crownless king

yet K content being one of many
to add to the others his *quiet* part
lend a little to the horns of plenty
to make it more a matter of heart

O-Yo-De-Lay-Hee-Hoing

on his two-year-old a satin-black
with forehead mark a whitish dot
a bridle Sears & Roebuck bought
he'd drive dogies to a dipping vat

aspiring to cords for alpine vocal
harmonizing vowels as cowhand
not with any falsetto of perpetual
boyhood no castrato's half a man

but to joy in the yodel of any age
from the pygmy African Austrian
Swiss Rumanian & Scandinavian
to campfires out in cactus & sage

hankered to warble as all the men
pictured singing on a silver screen
most often then a Gene Autry sort
no Pickens ever in a Republic part

closest thing to an improvised ride
mockingbird's 50 calls so accused
of copying squeaky gates any type
of peep its repertoire badly abused

while in Witter's Grenstone poems
he's declared the pilfering of tones
creates a medley out of a multitude
a single song hatched from a brood

while a chachalaca'll stick to "stac-
cato cadence" a mocker will "chirp
whistle stutter & yodel" as buzzard
wheels with just a silent dip & tack

could recognize a mellifluous dove
woodpecker's tap on a hollow trunk
learned each sound as any Audubon
a Longoria with his brushlands love

hearing her choir do "Precious Lord"
that joyful noise at Sunday's service
always choked up Alfreda Inglehart
K too attended the sanctified church

its swaying congregation patting feet
clapping hands in humid August heat
to hymns soldiering onward in Christ
in the *Elmer Gantry* film its cornetist

leads choir helped André Previn win
an Oscar for his lofty score & on *My
Fair Lady* a hard swinger as he'd fly
across his keys to drum-bass Friends

but traded jazz piano for a London
gig of Rachmaninoff works as con-
ductor of Sergei's *Symphony No. 3
Isle of the Dead* the *"Crag" Fantasy*

that '60 movie based on just a sole
Sinclair Lewis episode a repetitive
plot about its likable but seductive
preacher Lancaster in Elmer's role

but largely changed from the novel
like Sister Sharon played by pretty
Jean Simmons quitting the revival
or she says she will & even marry

yet persisting tent catches fire with
her inside Burt forgiving panicked
knocked her down rushing to save
sinful lives over which she prayed

when K's Pop would speak of God
he couldn't accept poor being good
if wealthy gained from fruits of evil
a heavenly hope made life tolerable

here on earth but said unworthwhile
lost religion found it all too political
compared it to booking agent who's
out for self not for sake of the muse

but's getting ahead has first to touch
his Sis Eva Lois' keyboard on which
she learned pieces attending Lincoln
High in Palestine played for bottling

companies for a Dr. Pepper of Waco
for Coca-Cola its weekly hour show
to promote its drink with a selection
of sight-read tunes Handy Ellington

she to prophesy K's always jumpin'
up & down to her music must mean
would grow up a Louis or a Gabriel
bright biblical high-toned archangel

K's "Mack the Knife" of '59 his own
rocking take on song of Weill-Brecht
the piece Papa Dip did with his direct
& unembellished New Orleanian tone

but before bop coming sharecrop bail-
ing of hay & alfalfa pulling boles scal-
ing with weights sacks two times long
as K & the boiling of cane & sorghum

herding a hundred head to local corral
begging handout for that peg-leg hobo
bound for Frisco spying oil lamp glow
tested first by his Mom forever cordial

from a white bum's yarns K's yearning
to ride the rods to the Mexicans' border
envisioning maybe Henrik Ibsen's *Peer
Gynt* heard "Hall of the Mountain King"

if he listened to Grieg's incidental *Suite*
in school his ears to ski dizzying slopes
of Norway's Gjendin ridge the ice floes
reindeer cracked & a Peer in hot pursuit

on "Minor's Holiday" Ken hanging on
to Anitra's theme as if some folksinger
hopped a freight & swung by its ladder
with rails clicked him to a distant town

after he'd watched the V-shaped flocks
honking high overhead as the Sunshine
Special blew lonesome across its tracks
he'd find a Bull Durham roll-your-own

that tramp's butt he'd smoke on the sly
since at home no tobacco no one drank
only watermelon under a star-filled sky
as bullfrogs sang to an ice cream crank

soaking up & absorbing nature's music
began with the rooster's morning crow
from their mud hole the grunt of a sow
with nightfall growls croaks & crickets

in spring a mateless mocker urging on
the one out there with a singing meant
for her alone outlined by a risen moon
his lyricless call "This Is the Moment"

in '58 K's rendition of Robin's words
in the same year his "Where Are You"
from that team of Adamson-McHugh
but had known their songs from birds

living six miles out had rarely bought
Fairfield paper as vagabonds brought
earlier news of Rangers busting a still
remembered chasing of a Villa or Dill-

inger a Baby Face or read special bul-
letins of the poem on Bonnie & Clyde
written in her blood before she'd died
of 10 G-men dead in Big D gun battle

knew a nearer death in old board well
from when a curious cat had fallen in
as the bucket rose so would the smell
with their water rotten dug a new one

knew too the windmill's metal clang
lifted precious liquid from far below
with curved turning fan blades sang
a pumping song made the cattle low

knew the ubiquitous plains machine
with self-governed centrifugal force
saved in drought cow sheep & horse
kept okra beans & other truck green

Go-devil or Mock if it wasn't theirs
was a "weathered gray-wood affair"
served him to write & title his tune
on Blue Note's *Whistle Stop* of '61

to Ira Gitler his tonal talk's romantic
but the tempo's far too fast & frantic
Philly Joe's skins so thunder & thud
it goes against setting a tender mood

maybe waited for her in shadows cast
by nighttime's one-eyed ogling moon
but "Sunset" with Hank Mobley's sax
sounds more evocative of rendezvous

with racism blatantly raising its head
in the street & anywhere would trade
were kept in their place labeled shift-
less said rotgut & dice their only drift

to this Kenny perhaps a bit oblivious
for luckily able to sell all his buckets
of beans okra tomatoes & fresh juicy
plums to Watt Parker owned the city

& as head of the telephone exchange
gave KD a penny to fetch any person
received a call its 3-short-1-long ring
he to answer even if not a Beethoven

in the 1890s on hauling corn by oxen
Watt letting horse & buggy pass him
but vowed one day he too would own
such a newfangled classy contraption

in later decades just two months after
the Market crash he'd open his dealer-
ship then have the gin & hospital built
better roads for selling his automobile

the banker-president of Fairfield State
chair of bond drive with world at war
attending '48 Convention as delegate
for Democrats & owned his 300-acre

plot with its weeds Ken had chopped
while his poppa handled for Mr. Watt
his four big young mules of top stock
& to drive his new International truck

delivering workers to the highway site
20 miles distant brought hardly wealth
but relief as two-lane neared the white
rented four-room house sat up on stilts

once living in one-room shotgun type
with along one side their rowboat tied
for spring when Trinity River to flood
cover feral animals & cattle with mud

panthers or bobcats killed the old cow
desperadoes in making their getaways
to ditch the stolen cars far out of town
in the land's lovely unending embrace

these the fragments he'd later jot down
rounding-ups led to his rhythmic drives
from calves cut out to notes like knives
not to carve but impart a sharper sound

delicious as Freestone County peaches
as stirring as Flash! Federal agents stop
interstate spree of cold-blooded thieves
satisfied in a way till he'd discover bop

with Bird & Cannonball ye-odle la-dee-
ing a cotton picker's very same melody
heard it on his dragging in his last sack
to weigh it & be paid a pittance of jack

with chases between a trumpet & tenor
non-violent exchanges with a rapid-fire
snare the alto bullets made none expire
but K's tones to slay boomed or tender

yet before they could to leave the farm
move to Austin take music by the horn
learn to go unthrown by buckaroo lines
bulldog etudes & scales in record times

Woodshedding

Ken's prodigious ear at five years old
could pick out keyboard boogies cold
& from Sis's 78s he could already tell
Louie on trumpet an equal of Gabriel

at ten the family agreed to let him live
with his uncle in the capital city where
in '03 student-poet John Lang Sinclair
wrote his "Eyes" sung by UT fans give

even now their Hook 'Em sign & in '31
at Hotel Driskill after a Texas freshman
heard the power & grace in Louis' horn
he faced his racism with shame & scorn

the Negro's notes as if from outer space
spinned in an orbit he had never known
& in '54 Charlie Black counsel for case
of Brown v. Board the seeds early sown

in '39 Sis'd convince their Daddy to buy
little Brother a 14-dollar horn so off-key
the bandmaster said he was never in tune
so got him a newer better his silver Conn

but soon the director had to send K home
ordered him to "get outa this music room
& don't come back" for stomping his feet
doing "Dipsy Doodle" to a swinging beat

for four long days disallowed in the class
dying to return then his folks took him in
for a serious talking to exacting a solemn
promise to straighten up fly right practice

every day to learn by heart a predictable
Sousa march's loud refrain its softer trio
& to stay in step out on the football field
yet with classes over Louie still his hero

for hours copying Dipper's hottest licks
from hymnal to alley & Storyville stalls
echoing back to him off pinewood walls
of his uncle's barn's seasoned acoustics

from Jericho tumbled by Joshua's siege
to opera shot mad-sweet pangs of key'd
cornets into Walt's epical belly & breast
wrenching ardors unaware he possessed

whirling him higher than a Ty's Uranus
& with her metal lips Emily to nonplus
her melodic bolts forever floating in air
as a balloon can lift or the pontoon pier

Job would hear God's whirlwind laugh
His terrible wrath in each trumpet blast
sniffing out a fight rejoiced in His rage
its dread bluster either to loose or cage

ca. 1358 B.C. the young Tutankhamen
dies on a desert hunt a death so sudden
then for afterlife embalmed in his tomb
with two trumpets in its art-filled room

when Misenus unsurpassed aeolian son
dared on his hollow horn to rival Triton
poppa Poseidon would drown his sound
surf thunder snuffing that brightness out

conch shells signaling sightings of ships
celibate Tibetans to blow the long pipes
Roland's oliphant warning great Charles
bugles for reveille taps retreat or charge

in more recent days slavery's obbligato
refitted the battle in the Negro spiritual
a shofar or hasosra fingered high or low
announcing priests enter & prostrate all

bull-voiced Nordic lur with its twisted S
bronze-shaped as if some mammoth tusk
ending in a flat ornamental disk a Danish
evidence of prechristian prehistory music

sea beasts of Grendel's mater startled by
thanes tooted arrival of Geat with troops
hunting horn din of Pearl's Green Knight
Chaucer's wooden *bemes* the village *poups*

Geoffrey's mock-epic of daun Russel fox
outwits Chauntecleer till opens his mouth
to brag when Fortune allows a slier cock's
comic escape a moral tale without a doubt

another rooster crowing the coming dawn
dispelling a specter of Hamlet father-king
horns braying response to Claudius' drink
flattery's profanation as sycophants fawn

Cleopatra's tart courier's senneted tidings
Tybalt blaring Juliet dead hatred's sidings
a tucket in *Henry Vth* sonance in *Macbeth*
the clamorous harbinger of blood & death

also in blank-verse cantos closer to home
in his *Historia de la Nueva México 1610*
Gaspar Pérez to chronicle clarions blown
as the *conquistadores* attack the Ácomen

in that unconquered fort of double peaks
a march to trumpets answer fife & drum
bent on a victory though braves outnum-
ber with water for just a couple of weeks

brasses vibrated from barnyard to castle
by bannered cherub or the Incorruptible
pealing endless reports of love or shame
vow or final reckoning forever proclaim

his chosen instrument storied in any age
yet never the same ever differs in length
cylindrical crook or tubular bell as page
flourishes a decree the herald a sentence

with invention of rotary & piston valves
concertos of Hummel Telemann Vivaldi
Fasch & of Haydns Joseph & Michael's
a Stravinsky puppet a Mahler symphony

in Respighi's *The Pines of Rome* a build-
up to legions tramping the Appian Way
returning victorious from the battlefield
with *bronces* bruiting rule of Roman *ley*

soloists Adolf Herseth & Maurice André
with a Sergei Nakariakov gaining entrée
Wynton Marsalis too to their inner circle
by circular-breathing a Molter or Purcell

Alison Balsom ringing Bach aria or suite
practicing barefooted in the window seat
her mouthpiece pressed to her softer lips
as petals where bee or hummingbird sips

yet his true precursor a Crescent City son
that legendary & unwaxed Buddy Bolden
called his children home with a European
horn prepared the way as did baptist John

whose descendants from Bunk to a racist
Nick LaRocca Papa Joe & Satchelmouth
Bix Bunny Diz & Miles each as an artist
to unite with his music a North & South

& last but not least on that list is yes KD
who heard of locals like a Teddy Wilson
Austin native left at six but in '35 Benny
Krupa & he together broke the color line

& Gene Ramey first on tuba a Royal Ace
in band of George Corley leader on 'bone
with Boots & His Buddies in San Antone
in KC in '32 double-jointed Gene on bass

in '42 kept time for pianist Jay McShann
Gus Johnson on Tyler drums Bird Parker
running scales Gene would feed his brain
before that needle need grew ever darker

its Cadillac tracks Ken to observe in years
to come & later at East 11th visited Victory
Grill served from '45 bop burgers & beers
earlier at 12th passed King-Tears mortuary

founded 1901 in '02 King to form a burial
associates first in U.S.A. but not to history
Ken listened then to an organ's unfunereal
holy-roller recovery of blues's living story

to hands clapped to that old-time religion
souls rocked in a bosom of hymnal swing
prepared him the way for his '64 playing
of Andrew's "Cadaver" later "Dedication"

forecasting his choruses on Horace Silver
Blue Note in '55 Ken's part on "Preacher"
a wa-wa exhortation wells up manly eyes
as congregation responds with amen cries

calls up his "Dorham's Epitaph" from '61
grateful for his brief marker he left behind
minute & 9 seconds of such uplifting pain
though later K to decide he would expand

the piece into score for strings some 60 or
70 instruments & even a Gunther Schuller
lauded "Fairy Tale" but never passed it on
for coming true with Lenny at the podium

long after his classes at East Austin's L.C.
Anderson High when Ken with his fellows
Buford Rip & Paris far out of earshot of B.
L. Joyce their band director would oppose

such improvising gathered at the Patterson
home at 1709 Washington Avenue for jam
sessions in Alvin's backyard Al later band
master remembered the "Tuxedo Junction"

of Erskine Hawkins Ken had loved to play
how he'd copied that trumpeter's bravado
style had caught him once in Boston blow-
ing with Billy Eckstine's band recalling K

as deep when lived near UT's Forty Acres
where he could hear the fight-song cheers
roared in that stadium for all-white teams
apartheid games he could view in dreams

yet satisfied being in this new-found land
while Garvey took a Liberia-bound stand
neither Andrew nor K ever seeming bitter
if both too nice each survived as the fitter

but if to attend a white school unpermitted
would go to Wiley College in piney woods
in Marshall that first of academic institutes
West of the River where Mel Tolson pitted

his debating team against & defeated USC
if KD ever read the poet's *Harlem Gallery*
how'd he take those lines on Jelly & Satch
the verses on jazz as a marijuana of blacks

or the Mel sonnet on learning & ignorance
made chemistry his major but grade denies
he stood in the field a "Ghost of a Chance"
pure fantasy or had he told little white lies

hoped to follow in Henderson's footsteps
Smith's too both of them trained chemists
Fletcher's B.S. from Atlanta Willie's Fisk
but later each sticking to the notes in clefs

K reporting too he had majored in physics
but in cal & periodic table bottom of class
yet if passed no courses his transcript lists
his differential & atomic bop will ever gas

in '40 he'd enroll too late to join the band
sat with Roy Porter outside the dining hall
listening as Collegians rehearsed Bertrand
Adams director then but in '41 "Wild Bill"

Davis who in '55 arranged Count's *April
in Paris* with the trombone section leader
Henry Coker who had gone to their other
college with Bishop then still in Marshall

while at Wiley Ken washing pots & pans
jamming for chicks sat on his dorm-room
bed & on getting caught nearly sent home
saved by his having taken Eddie Preston's

chair needed for coming Collegians' tour
playing dances battling with other outfits
traveled to Dallas & down to Port Arthur
up to Beaumont Midland Cowtown Paris

Hoagy's "Stardust" he arranged for band
the first KD made of his galaxy of charts
with their motifs inspired by many a land
& some would travel him to unseen parts

in the second year with its surprise attack
FDR denounced on radio the sneaky Japs
his infamy speech & after it draft & death
to big-band era & its jitter-bugging youth

when KD & his roomy Roy would each go
his separate way though later in the decade
Bird hiring Roy on drums then KD to blow
one to record in '46 the other to start in '48

& as he had in Wiley's band would replace
Bird's trumpet player & yet no simple case
of one greenhorn student traded for another
for would have to assume the coveted chair

of Miles no less his sound Ken went to hear
or did it's said from Austin after hearing tell
of Davis' St. Louis work with Eddie Randle
his soft delicate lines grapevined far & near

K's army tour prior to a Bird quintet tenure
& then free-lanced once his G.I. adventure
ended in honorable discharge after surgeon
botched appendectomy & with his pension

to attend in '43 the Gotham Music School
scuffling writing arrangements doing what-
ever it took going West with Russ Jacquet
with Frank Humphries in '44 then "Kool"

in '47 with Mary Lou & next Art Blakey
in his Octet Kaleem tenor Shihab on alto
December 27 on 2nd take of "Bop Alley"
K to outdo his own "The Thin Man" solo

earlier in '46 meeting Miles at Minton's
there too Fats Navarro who invited Ken
to sit in anytime & even earlier had Diz
audition him for bop's first big-band gig

hired in '45 stayed long as it would last
taking Gillespie's lessons arranging too
with the Ellington touch or tried at least
yet admitted had little success could du-

plicate if not Duke sort of what Diz'd do
said in writing knew the sound was after
& slowly over the years produced a slew
of songs some 80 listed in BMI's register

heard Bird at Minton's & after Dizzy dis-
banded took Fats's seat in Billy Eckstine
band found work in a score of groups his
home on 157th St. when Bird would sign

him up on Miles saying K'd fill his shoes
how hope to yet in a stint at Royal Roost
Ken to prove as Traill the Brit trumpeter
would later write few bop partners better

& already Ken had shown he could keep
up with the likes of Sonny Stitt on a Bud
Powell date of August 23rd not any creep
on their '46 sides no single piece of crud

he none on Bud's "Serenade to a Square"
& on Powell's bouncy "Bebop in Pastel"
KD's solo opens with bursting out all rar-
ing to go & here to stay for no brief spell

& wails too on B's classic "Fool's Fancy"
contrasting his string of with fewer notes
& on K's own "Bombay" his solo quotes
Kern's "Ol' Man River" to do it all in '60

with his quintet when tenor Jimmy Heath
& pianist Kenny Drew take it slow at first
& then cut loose with a Mississippi keeps
a-rollin' as the stevedore despite his hurts

& on K's other tune his "Blues in Bebop"
Sonny shows how much he owes to Bird
BP's all over keyboard roaming non-stop
then Ken opens with a phrase ever heard

at Xmas time but here even in dog days'
heat preparing by quote of "Santa Claus
Is Coming to Town" for the larkish ways
of Parker's wit still gives a listener pause

on September 5th with Navarro on Kenny
Clarke's 52nd St. Boys' recording session
Bud & Sonny again another rebop lesson
begins with two Monk tunes "Epistrophy"

& of course "52nd Street Theme" the first
with no chorus by Ken or Fats just a half
by Stitt also in St. Nick lick well-versed
& on hearing it later a hipster will laugh

after ensemble has stated 52nd St. theme
the soloist Ray Abrams leads off backed
by trumpets tenorist next delivers dream
of a dynamic drive & then KD if in fact

not Fats as some believe but not Leif Bo
& Theo attesting it is Kenny all the way
with his finest solo on this '46 date as K
plays with power but too with lyric flow

Navarro's greater on "Oop Bop Sh'Bam"
the tenor coming on again like dynamite
on "Rue Chaptal" Fats more secure than
Ken who's less mature relaxed articulate

yet growing still & on September 6th KD
with Fats & The Bebop Boys do "Boppin'
a Riff" when he shows there's no stoppin'
him now a cat slow or fast ain't no fraidy

on Navarro's "Fat Boy" K's called clum-
sy but only on take one for on the second
a single chorus just outstanding as he rips
& sings a contrast to Fats's fluent triplets

"Everything's Cool" & it is on this piece
where Ken turns in a "convincing" break
with thrilling double-time runs can wake
the dead yet let them rest better in peace

& on "Webb City" BP "unconventional"
tune looks ahead to his dance of infidels
KD & Fats adding the keen two-trumpet
fills if K can't match a smooth FN triplet

will after study with such bop professors
from boyhood blessed with hayseed ears
could hear the diminished in a minor riff
& would learn lyrics would come to live

Bird Chasing

Confidence! thy name is Kenny Dorham
how else take over for Miles in a premier
unit of that post-war day no tinge of fear
in offering himself as the sacrificial lamb

December 25th of '48 on the airways with
"Half Nelson" tricky Davis tune on which
K holds his own no hitch his pitches turns
all in tune dovetailing in time with Bird's

but KD's own conceptions still unformed
as he rushes about trying too hard to keep
up with Diz's or Fat Girl's historical horn
their scalar flashes stratospherically deep

then's nearer his melodic self on Berlin's
perennial hit a call-in request as if a joke
yet Bird on "White Christmas" brightens
spirits with a bit of a "Jingle Bells" quote

if Ken to stumble some still finds his way
& will give himself time as a patient man
but when Bird claims he drew in advance
a hundred dollars out of his monthly pay

K cuts short the argument & pulls a blade
says he'll draw Chazz's blood if isn't paid
Yard replies as he forks up a rightful sum
"just seeing where you was coming from"

did Ken think Bird's brilliant solos came
from his baleful habits the way he'd play
from a lax life & believe very often fame
ungained in living right doing so anyway

on "Jumpin' with Symphony Sid/Bebop"
K excels at its faster time but isn't on top
of his game off now on New Year's night
from a rushed execution reduces thought

& on "Slow Boat to China" though plays
too many notes yet reveals a warmer side
& Bird with his Chinese music criticized
by Cab who sang it too will simply daze

K's solo here has a cleaner shape & ends
in a type of tying up he'd clearly learned
under Bird's instructive wings & extends
by taking in more feeling a flying earned

on the first night of '49 "East of the Sun"
follows after "Ornithology" a bebop pun
on Bird's nickname then Diz's "Groovin'
High" both these tunes so tried & proven

played here Loren says with CP abandon
while Ken's still immature though blends
with Bird as well as any & on solos fends
for himself in bringing in the little he can

& if on that ballad with the rest of its title
"and West of the Moon" K isn't as lyrical
as Bird when he's stating with his special
graces its dreamy theme oh a blest recital

still Ken adds a part's lovely too at times
as on entering at first he's kept the mood
romantic but up high he suddenly climbs
to reach for feeling at an Andean altitude

on the 15th on "Scrapple From the Apple"
Ken works his way to the Birdsong seeds
his shifts & turns abrupt as Al Haig feeds
the crazy chords moldy figs just to baffle

few could ever match K velocity on "Be-
bop" or on this Charlie tune his dexterity
his technical wizardry but such only goes
so far one needs too soulful highs & lows

on "Hot House" Bird & K are into quotes
B chasing the weasel around the mulberry
bush & each weaving his lines from every
unlikely source as if sowed onions & oats

hear maybe Grieg but pop songs for sure
yet the titles escape with so many carried
in their capacious heads & though buried
still the notes endure Death can't immure

on the 22nd Bird sings "Oop Bop Sh'bam"
with all his band then with mouthpiece in
blows its riff sings again & blows it again
then changes the tune as quick as shazam

& rides to the *Paleface* theme with buck-
board bounce toted guns toes cacti-stuck
& then where Bird left off K's picked up
& swings on his mount spurs into gallop

next up again it's "Scrapple" but amaz-
ing more so now for Bird fully displays
his aural prowess & did it make K have
his doubts a bruised ego needed a salve

intimidated by Parker's affective power
did Ken then consider giving it up quit-
ting & turning to another career felt fit-
ter for & thoughts of music all run sour

could well have been but fact not fiction
reveals a tale of KD determined as Tyco
studied his stars K the Bird's instruction
from anonymous to the Broadway show

applied his learning then & in later years
if wasn't before would become a magpie
attracted as Bird by any sound in his ears
others' bright or benighted tunes any cry

on the 25th he took a break joined forces
with vibes of "Bags" Milt Jackson that is
& "Klook" on drums Kenny Clarke nom
de guerre for their session different from

recording dates Ken accustomed to since
this with vibraharp tenor trumpet French
horn tenor bass & drums in combination
produce the strangest "Conglomeration"

as that title tune of Bags would sum it up
though not meant in any pejorative sense
his "Roll 'em Bags" in need of no defense
as it mixes Ken's mute his straight or cup

with his open bell for a solo best of three
yet maybe the one on "Bruz" even better
each kicked on by Klook & bassist Curly
Russell's solid beat their get up go-getter

& yet still not Bags's matchless affiliation
the one would find with a 30-year MJQ
of John Percy Connie & himself came to-
gether formed its own more perfect union

& K too still to know his ideal synergism
& yet said playing with Bird his ambition
for many a year though as the saying goes
once had the much desired has its sorrows

not that then or later Kenny ever laments
his time with Chazz but seems so at ease
with the Jackson grab bag of instruments
even Frenchy & unshabby tenor'll please

then January 29th "Groovin' High" again
but now the Bird giving K a longer leash
as if so happy to have him back lets Ken
get the one horn solo his range increased

on February 5th a muted K's "Apple" not
quite so satisfying as on Milt's "Roll'em"
but on "Barbados" sounds like hot to trot
on "Salt Peanuts" cutting a flawless gem

come February 12th it's a burnt-out case
for "Apple" has lost its sauce after night-
after-night though in their two-bar chase
Bird & K still polish it up halfway bright

in March KD still scrappling the "Apple"
but muted to good advantage & "Cheryl"
on the 12th even better since his emergent
self now coming through his singing bent

earlier on the 5th not floating quite so free
without the piano though Bird more spon-
taneous forecasting later Rollins Freedom
even as Loren writes Ornette's "Dee Dee"

on 12th CP with septet "Chasin' the Bird"
shows none could then can now catch up
to Charlie & Kenny's even come in third
behind Bags' sparkling solo as runner-up

in early spring of '49 will travel to Cream
City where Bird's out to paint Milwaukee
red with to KD each chorus more supreme
just sits there & listens to Charlie's beauty

when Bird asks Ken what he wants to play
"Circus" he says & Charlie sings its theme
then high-wire act with rhythm section lay-
ing down the beat for bop's acrobatic team

the same quintet will soon be off to France
& in advance all had tendered applications
for "Passport" & "Visa" titles of the band's
recorded sides of Bird's own compositions

happy pieces reflective of visionary smiles
thoughts of a far-off scenery foreign words
after Ken & his packed-ready nod to Miles
Tommy Turk on his trombone rarely heard

perhaps too Bird intended such contrafacts
as homage to Frenchmen embracing blacks
or to those who found open arms & stayed
dropping bombs Kenny Clarke first played

Paris in May its International Jazz Festival
Ken recording minus Parker's peerless sax
"replaced" by James Moody on tenor Max
Roach on drums Tommy Potter bass & Al

Haig's piano on tunes include "Baby Sis"
Ken's number where he's into something
other than just bebop phrases as here fits
in silent spaces lullaby lines softly cooing

more so on "Tomorrow" his ballad's time
changed from "Yesterdays" based it upon
first of two K versions of Kern's '33 song
into its bottle pouring his own new wine

for Parker Quintet concert at Salle Pleyel
Bird revisits a tune he had made his own
"Out of Nowhere" recalls how unknown
his sound had been whose since can rival

not just his gymnastic flips twists & turns
nor the "Happy Birthday" personal quote
but as Potter's solo ends Bird's each note
potent with a meaning & a feeling burns

& in slowing K now saying so much more
shapes his long lines to make better sense
knows has gotten through as the audience
applauds & its shouting approaches a roar

in every take of "Salt Peanuts" KD shows
is Jack nimble & quick over a candlestick
on "52nd St. Theme" he's mining melodic
veins as Bird with his "Buttons & Bows"

& would again on Festival's final Sunday
during that all-out jam on "Allen's Alley"
dust-caked disc of which Michel'd rescue
from a friend's attic with soapsuds renew

another preserved with a "52nd St. Theme"
saved both & above all a line-up of greats
from Byas Bechet & Bird's sexiest breaks
to trumpeters Aime Bill Miles Lips & Ken

though in notes Mark Gardner's uncertain
it's KD solos just before the Bird comes in
yet who else could it be of those on the list
after Byas surely it's Coleman's *sui generis*

swing reminding of his '36 expatriate work
with Django & Grappelli following records
of '34 with Fats & His Rhythm on "Dream
Man" ever marvelous la crème de la crème

Sidney's superb on soprano but capital city
is Charlie's oyster then tape cuts off luckily
not before he alludes to "I'm Gonna Move
to the Outskirts of Town" Basie's '42 blues

by year's end KD moving too Red Rodney
taking his place after Bird let him go yet K
not one for holding a grudge as Red to tell
K'd been understanding & even "beautiful"

& as his successor foretold K continued on
establishing a unique & vital voice his own
in sinc with saxophonists Rollins to ’Trane
earning sturdy respect if but minor acclaim

Westering

in '50 quit Atlantic lit out for Pacific
debouching in reverse as Walter said
like Huck or a Forty-Niner but head-
ing out a century late to strike it rich

panning nuggets prior to Napa wine
not picking rows as Okie & migrant
but for a wife & two daughters sign-
ing on at a Republic's aviation plant

an ammunition dump over in Vallejo
in Oakland at the U.S. medical depot
later would part-time for a Jack Frost
sugar refinery any job to pay the cost

of clothes & rent not unhappy giving
up the horn as he needed to get away
split the scene & try the scenic living
escape an after hours laboring by day

if not Polonius believed Mingus' line
on either coast one should be oneself
many K said wouldn't restock a shelf
hollered Freedom! Avant-Garde! fine

by him not to whine stuck to his guns
never to envy or covet fellow Texians
stars at Hermosa Beach in a Kenton's
"New Sounds" or over at the Trade Winds

Bird Baker & Texas bass Harry Babasin
for KD not missing spotlight or crowds
feeling lucky being distant from addiction
fool's gold lifts then drops from clouds

on leaving Bird in '49 Davis gave birth
to cool a Rugolo coin for Gerry's "Jeru"
& "Rocker" Miles' "Deception" Lewis'
"Rouge" with Evans's theories at work

with trumpet star Gil aligned & altered
the energy levels boosted fused bop el-
ements for creating a 9-piece ensemble
orchestrated so light no soloist faltered

influence followed as Mulligan himself
went West his desert boots as "Walking
Shoes" & there's Shorty Rogers talking
Nonet too who beside his Giants an elf

his long trumpet lines like K's although
if not so daring nor intriguing yet swing
barely breathing so intent on his "Popo"
& on his "Apropos" so hell-bent to fling

caution to the winds to whirl as a dervish
then Jimmy Giuffre arriving from Dallas
huffing his tenor ever steady no nervous-
irvis rather his folksy "easy way" relaxes

yet drives home its simple loaded phrase
in '57 improvising *Suspensions'* notation
of tom-tom figure but first in '51 parleys
his '47 Herman hit into another iteration

of "Brothers" theme his "Four Mothers"
with Jolly Rogers in swashbuckling form
JG a patch-eyed pirate takes no prisoners
prodded onto plank by Art's hooked arm

& all in fun as Hawes & Pepper pour it on
ignoring cross-boned yelling madcap crew
as K loads shells gunpowder a medication
pushing dollies with meantime his embou-

chure slack doesn't practice lacks contact
with mouthpiece would touch it but's four
to feed has to eschew it & to face the fact
family's first yet an urge to more & more

while Ornette a fellow native low in L.A.
for an unheated garage cleans her kitchen
& baby-sits kids walks miles just to sit in
if he does asked "who taught you to play"

told to "learn the changes out-of-tune fool"
knows it isn't true & his keening the same
in '59 he & Ken together at Lenox School
teachers of the art before Coleman's fame

his soloing on his "Sphinx" a master class
of roaming the plains & trusting one's ear
its western pitches & slurs so hard to hear
for any afraid to venture into his fenceless

range's unknown sound foreign & strange
Kenny's own "D.C. Special" nothing new
his student group performing not yet up to
his then outmoded bop K chose to arrange

but to take no chorus himself a selflessness
allowed beginners their moment in the sun
as did some others Giuffre Roach & Lewis
a FreeFactory CD documents the occasion

K known too to share equally the solo time
on albums he'd make on his trips back east
in the years before his basking in that lime-
light rubbing innovators' elbows & at least

if traded no four-bars with harmolodic king
& unaware of him when the two struggling
to survive on golden shores assured a place
in pantheon bearing Ornette's name & face

neither a part of Frisco's jazz-poetry scene
Ferlinghetti doing "Junkman's Obbligato"
to a local quintet his City Lights printing
after *Howl* Parra's *Antipoems* F lifting "no

bird sang" from sonnet 73 some Eliot Stein
& Whitman made Yeats' "Isle of Innisfree"
into Manisfree from epitaph McMurtry
taking for *Horseman, Pass By* its final line

in '61 K to cut *Inta Somethin'* Pacific Jazz
taping him at the San Francisco Workshop
with altoist Jackie McLean student of bop-
pers from Bird to Mingus the angry Chazz

but in '51 Ken not as Giuffre a Lighthouse
All-Star joining in summer of '56 the MJQ
& recorded at Berkshires Music Inn venue
yet in '52 K with Monk pre-Charlie Rouse

for "Skippy" & "Carolina Moon" coming
on strong a sort of hard-bop line removed
from Giuffre's "Fun" & a Lewis "Fugue"
in classical drive Milt's 'harp a-humming

on all four Monk tunes recorded May 30th
K to do himself proud soloing on "Hornin'
In" & the lovely "Let's Cool One" & with
his ensemble work as bright as the mornin'

light as he joins with Lou Donaldson alto
& Lucky Thompson tenor on Thelonious'
rarely played his "intricate & treacherous"
"Skippy" his waltzed southern lunar glow

in Ken's later bag as *Down Beat* reviewer
to depict "odd but elegant" Monkish attire
of green sharkskin suit black shoes leather
skull cap & high priest's solo catching fire

in '60 K pictured on stage a Newport rebel
with Ornette & his white plastic sax beside
the bass of Mingus whose own Debut label
to issue K's first album in '53 with his side-

men Jimmy Heath tenor Percy bass Clarke
on drums Walter Bishop piano as K blows
& goes he & Jim in the flow on "Osmosis"
& to bassist "Darn That Dream"'s no lark

Percy ever serious & on "Ruby, My Dear"
K slows it down & then on "Be My Love"
speeds up with his patented staccato touch
Latin beat on "I Love You" his "An Oscar

for Oscar" the K original started things off
all proving him a hat-trick magician of bal-
lad or alla-breve rabbit stunts adroit at soft
to loud high low fast slow swing to chorale

in '52 as well with Percy's bass in a Sextet
Donaldson as leader his 1st LP he in hunt
as others to inherit Parker's throne a front-
line of Lou's alto Gee trombone K trumpet

Matthew a Texan too with his bone's quick
on the draw as K could be & each's release
smooth as cool-handed gunslinger squeeze
on "Caracas" Gee the faster if have to pick

in '58 at George Wein's Rhode Island Fest
Giuffre filmed with own then featured Trio
Hall guitar Brookmeyer 'bone a subtle brio
"The Train and the River" the leader's best

at that rival Rebel concert Ken only caught
by recorders as his piano backed up Abbey
Lincoln singing her "Bizness" some said K
absconded with its funds perish the thought

generous to a fault charge should rather be
so think of K's daughters Keturah & Leslie
wife Rubina their later girls LeJuine Evette
& Lamesha this last perhaps Ken's favorite

for when was three he'd title a tune for her
described by Ken in his notes to *Page One*
the first album with Joe Henderson's tenor
their '63 session the two as if father & son

his girls to visit by train Uncles & Aunties
to arrive as city-bred & prim young ladies
August Texas heat so primitive they cried
from stickers & as headless chickens died

to NYC-born mother did K's "Stage West"
mean a thing if not ever in his dusty boots
never kicked around in his Post Oak roots
could she find in Giuffre's "Pony Express"

an appeal K shared for Jim's loping rhythm
or the least in his "California Here I Come"
but maybe could take his "The Quiet Time"
if it made K's *Quiet Kenny* pop in her mind

though never named a song for her another
strong & tender mate juggling roles mother
housekeeper wage earner a keeper of home
fires burning a safe house a warm welcome

other women making do sewing patchwork
quilts of artful design bright African colors
sold to casual buyers or museums' curators
without any alimony deadbeat fathers shirk

an irresponsibility in no way meant to refer
to Ken's case nor a Monk's his "Crepuscule
with Nellie" written & titled for his skillful
wife handled his tours trusted in her answer

if asked her opinion & as falcon Thelonious
turned perned in gyres would buy him a bus
plane or train ticket cook for his men bacon
& eggs Diz's too named her tune "Lorraine"

K's "Fragment" ends before Rubina's career
back in "great smog" of NYC its night shifts
of changing sheets with its roll-overs & lifts
empty bedpans injection given in hip or rear

his girls grown used to a metropolitan speed
crowded sidewalks high rises higher fashion
faster speech another scenery a greater need
to keep up with & have a piece of the action

difficult to feel attraction for his hostile land
dried creek beds burned grass coiling snakes
a whirring locust drove them mad said takes
natives to put up with racism wouldn't stand

never the twain shall meet can still hold true
despite the golden spike hammered together
east & west the ring not in his nose no fetter
if not his musical muse she'd seen it through

put up with his irregular hours tours abroad
home with reek of nightclub smoke thought
up & gave him the "Fairy Tale" title for ex-
tension of his "Epitaph" five of her own sex

while Kenny even though he'd tied the knot
faithful to a coast-to-coast wedding of blues
& gospel with its have hard-bop cool-to-hot
orient-occident horn-will-travel Good News

after from time to time having returned to record
with those espoused a new faith in the funky soul
its torment & simplicity & the down-home chord
to cook with the Latin-tinged recipe of Jelly Roll

Ken if ungiven to visions or visitations of a hard-
boiled hard-core melancholy sort now entered his
minor mode "sayin'-something" more-expressive
phase encapsulated partly by a '60 title *Eastward*

Ho! KD & Houston native Harold Land's reunion
in NYC from when in '55 tenor'd vacated his seat
in the Max Roach Quintet & left for L.A. & when
in '57 Harold & Ken then with Roach would meet

for Herb Geller's *Fire in the West* & its "Jitterbug
Waltz" a happy Waller tune right for cuttin' a rug
as the races mix & revisit Fats's swinging thirties
updating its ¾ time with a bopster's witty flurries

their notes exploring "Here's What I'm Here For"
of Arlen & Gershwin by then K's lyricism warm
& wise an accurate attack & clearer tone a mirror
of his secure arrival after years down on the farm

his Big Apple sojourn of '53 for his Birdland date
when Blakey Silver Donaldson & Ramey open up
with KD's "An Oscar for Oscar" Art's skins erup-
ting with rolls & rimshots until KD is out the gate

racing not for a finish line but to reach by his runs
the deeper pockets of their Bop ore's richest veins
as Lou stakes out each high-grade deposit remains
quick Silver's keys panning unclaimed mountains'

ice-cold streams for all they're worth even though
recording quality so poor only Gene's baptist bass
is mostly clear while both horns & Horace's piano
fade out at times in the nightclub's crowded space

on the Silver tune "Split Kick" Lou seems to float
to rotate 180° as if in kung fu then land on his feet
after which Ken begins lyric then is suddenly fleet
as his lungs & lips deliver his solid note-after-note

but what is so great about such a Telly Savalas act
William Hazlitt wrote of Indians juggled four balls
at once even revolved like planets behind the back
when few can even manage three his Cavanaugh's

unrivalled fives-court games with spectator shouts
"stood him in stead of a posterity's unheard voice"
the power to fill a public's mind not dextrous louts
but those whose energy can move to feeling Joyce

Shakespeare Michelangelo or Walt who all impart
their unlimited thought has taken imaginative hold
& this may include the musician's cogitating heart
pumping in ears sound ideas even dearer than gold

in August '54 Ken in NYC for a Prestige date with
Sonny Rollins produced his hard-swinging *Moving
Out* along with Hope Heath & Blakey the grooving
rhythm section backing trumpet & tenor prove kith

& kin wax eloquent on "Solid" as if a family blues
pushing & prodding one another to let it all loose
& on "Swingin' for Bumsy" both blowing & going
hell for leather & only with "Silk n' Satin" slowing

by December '54 back East to stay & with Blakey
he's tight again as in '45 had been in that Gillespie
band in Billy Eckstine's too & together later in '47
in Art's Octet whose Messengers name he'd given

first to his mystic unit of 17 turbaned goateed men
though Ken not a member of that next year's partly
Moslem group with Sahib Shihab & Musa Kaleem
changed slave to Arabic appellations as Shafi Hadi

his own from Curtis Porter their two from Edmund
Gregory & Orlando Wright the latter an Al Cooper
Savoy Sultan before William Evans'd play on tour
as Yusef Lateef or Sun Ra'd shorten Sonny Blount

or Cassius Clay'd convert his into Muhammad Ali
the greatest with fists & rhymes like "rope a dope"
"thrilla in Manila" conversion inspired by the hope
heard in Malcolm X's words not the autobiography

Haley wrote after El-Hajj Malik El-Shabazz broke
with the Nation of Islam's head Elijah Muhammad
for whose Black Muslims Malcolm as Malik spoke
until he left the movement & fanatic followers had

him gunned down shot for disavowal of racial hate
while KD whatever form it took would never allow
belief system agenda either right or left to separate
any would make music together in the here & now

as when in '47 Sahib & Musa had joined with Ken
for his "The Thin Man" featured his fanfare phrase
he'd open with then his soaring solo in vindication
of Bird's inviting him to take Miles' coveted place

the "Bop Alley" alternate displaying KD's flawless
rapid-fire period style but by '54 went with Horace
& Art into a bop called hard more unadorned simp-
ler chords & low-down gutbucket lexicon no hemp

Mobley's tenor into darker-toned modes Rosenthal
reports from his Jewish point of view's love for all
such blues to bring fewer motifs to their softer boil
less hard-edged than a Bird's hardly so labyrinthal

that altered word recalls how K unlike those others
never changed his name except to switch the letters
in McKinley dropping Mc i & l to leave just Kenny
as for hope of heaven's unveiled virgins hadn't any

as far as hindsight eyes can see or any ears surmise
may never know if K'd ever read Emerson Address
at the Divinity School's graduation class's exercise
essayed then the evils of his church made manifest

but it seems K'd known it from early on & rejected
miracles meant for converting men as "profanation
of the soul" & found as Blake did services infected
preferred god in man as Waldo did & no mediation

on December 13th Silver & Messengers to expound
as Ira Gitler says on seven Horace songs plus Hank
Mobley's "Hankerin'" the tenorist's punning prank
with which in going along the others long to sound

uneccentric flexible emotive & inventive as a quin-
tet could ever wish Art's drums volcano rumblings
Hank's sinewy tenor Ken's pungent horn rooted in
the leader's Gospel fingers Doug's walking strings

unison on "Stop Time" on "Doodlin'" whole tones
fooling around with staccato humor 12-to-the-bar
all this found in Ira's notes for the '54-'55 sessions
needn't reinvent the wheel can depend on Gitler

& others' trenchant depictions for a lot of the fun
of long play & compact discs to read those once-
in-a-lifetime liners if not a paragraph or sentence
will ever put into words a music's perfect diction

"Room 608" that pianist's Horatian ode he wrote
to his being on the road far from home hotel stay
where in Ira's words seldom is KD heard to play
as fluent & assured the best of Diz & Davis both

of "Hippy" Ira states Blakey knocks on the door
& all fall in but it sounds on "Creepin' In" more
as if they're slinkin' about in a slow funky burn
& sermonize on "To Whom It May Concern"

with "The Preacher" biggest of benediction hits
where Horace's backbeat reaches to an old-time
barrelhouse barroom feeling made Ira reminisce
of an "I've Been Working on the Railroad" line

reminds too how those sang a chain-gang chant
added to yet never knew & could ever ill afford
78 LP or CD player for digging a Horace chord
& what good'd it do for a black hungry indigent

while the white hipster ate it up in a luxury pad
is there no fair play or justice in the land of jazz
yet lifts who's heard or listens to that '55 ballad
its "Yesterdays" of November 23rd where K has

what Jelly says he needed & Oliver's doctor had
where at Café Bohemia as Art Horace & Doug
Watkins back him up KD'll climb from his sad
singing to double-timing can give the heart a tug

then all up-tempo on "Just One of Those Things"
with Ken leading the way Art goading with press
rolls & his sticks-on-snare-rim motivic clickings
for their mike-announced Blue Note cooking ses-

sion with reticent Mobley that label's rising star
at simmer point in a pot put on but not that car-
toon sort of a cannibal bone-through-nose heats
the cauldron with hapless missionary as his eats

in between sets Mobe reclusive in beat-up Buick
smoking alone any talking done with his laconic
horn releases a nonchalant softer rounder sound
tenor & trumpet conversing running up or down

his & KD's voices placid on "I Waited For You"
the last lines "spoken as one" Hank if wordless
an introvert his sense of rhythm something new
to Dexter endearingly Hankenstein but to Davis

after 'Trane his phrasing banal & yet reputation
the bubble he'd never sought his '60 *Soul Station*
considered his claim to fame though Messenger
dates with Art Horace KD & Doug'll still prefer

even hearing that tinny nearly out-of-tune piano
Horace's heroical hand ripples from high to low
blue notes & chords from that genome diaspora
spread like fingers out of Africa to arctic aurora

holding first to stone-age tools a handle gripped
thonged to their flint head rhythmically chipped
already indications of man's integrating circuits
blowing glass turning spears into pruning hooks

using tuning fork as two-pronged attack brasses
& saxes in pitched battle for emitting mellowest
moans or joyous tones by vibrating reeds or lips
on metal cups a hand tossing touchdown passes

too often grenades or now planting deadly IEDs
instead of gut strung to sing mallets to hammer
so wire will ring a sword beaten into plowshare
toes on pedals prolong or soften chords of keys

back to Silver's ivories black & white with bass
treble sharp flat major minor in each hand right
left or both at once stretches them to encompass
the diapason from deep to an harmonious height

message too through bronze tube & even further
back to axon's brain synapse a neural transmitter
in contact with dendrite's chemical receptor fires
its electrical signal to the nervous system inspires

feet to tap hands clap lips buzz lung pump tongue
in touching the roof to trill articulate exploded air
fingers & thumb chip an obsidian flake in rhythm
for cutting wind holes in swan the vulture feather

flute & pipe together with striking of lithophones
in ice-age painted cave stalagmites & wing bones
to appeal to or appease the unseen god commune
with ursine or archer's constellation sun or moon

extended as von Weber an invitation to the dance
kicking up heels stomping of dry or muddy banks
yelling chanting humming through harp-like cords
shells too for feelings & fears millenia later words

but first a bonobo hoot its staccato primal scream
synchronized calls & noisy bouts from communal
cries rang tree to tree prior to descent to a bipedal
magical savanna life turned on that hair-loss gene

brought sweating from long-distance chasing after
faster rest-deprived deer beginnings from long ago
by way of gibbon gorilla laughing chimp to Homo
habilis Lucy's Australopithecinus brainier ergaster

the wider polyglossal canal of Neanderthals piping
capacity for sound perception & inner ear vocaliza-
tion to hyoid bone velum & tongue one other muta-
tion by design or chance led to letter note & typing

to "Decifering the Message" Hank's bonus number
not on the LP of '55 but on the compact disc of '87
tenorist unlocking with the key he's in burnt-umber
to dark-skinned blues an ocher stripe as decoration

on artefacts unearthed in Blombos Cave pigmenta-
tion telling a tribal tale of collective hunting ghost
exorcized by skin cosmetics color lighter by eleva-
tion or climatic change long story of bias & boast

banding together to scavenge a predator kill these
for watching nodding heads patting soles keeping
time to their dozen tones varied with rare repeats
high or low a slow fast sorrowful joyful weeping

in Ken's following of the reedman's lead is more
into his speed than Hank's motivic tracks broken-
chord snapped-twig grass-imprinted trail a token
of one who's gone ahead playing this way before

KD even running as a puma or gazelle can quote
"Salt Peanuts" & into his solo in his own "Prince
Albert" inserts the woodpecker cartoon call note-
for-note not a showboat but making perfect sense

Ken's Martin ax if no primitive stone implement
no descendant of a swung prehistoric instrument
akin to chimpanzee stick probes termite mounds
his of brass for its dragging out of tastier sounds

than cicada whirs or buzzing from a hole in bark
a tree's honied hive's horde of bees & the queen
it guards as K's warm tone swarms tornado dark
now sweeter & fleeter on his tune "The Theme"

& on soloing he takes in his "Minor's Holiday"
a high-velocity series of calisthenic twists leaps
vaults & jumping jacks then a stop-time display
with Art's drumming all the company he keeps

the rimshots urging him to soar as cymbal burst
punctuates K's isometrics & then the rest join in
returning to end this number's too brief vacation
release from earthbound limitation internal hurts

transcended through a hearing relays its message
to encephal receptors translate transmissions live
on audio wave vinyl or disc stars gone for an age
beaming brightly preterit rays as if were yet alive

for travel back in time two notes enough to enter
a folk dance in Bartók style or *Der Rosenkavalier*
its familiar waltz opening-bar French horn signal
another in the *Merry Pranks* of Till Eulenspiegel

though Edison by magnet embossed Mary's song
first on paper disk then wired in cylinder grooves
Berliner in his modulating a lateral disc improves
its analogue ancestor just as jazz is coming along

whether working together or each alone inventive
men bequeathed recording horn a stylus a rhythm
mass-produced of blues men blew who not to live
on to survive in playbacks of rpms & bits to come

as KD tone reverberates in homes he never knew
its phrases still ringing in rooms of a faithful few
can tell them apart in solo or played with a group
his fingerprint his signature sound none can dupe

Prophesying

if a steady gig gathers moss it sets the food
on dinner plates & lowers the marital stress
would keep that vow yet his music mistress
too & he kept them both in a mellow mood

then parts ways with Art did he not foresee
indulging a craving to form & lead his own
quintet would become another rolling stone
was it in the cards or had Ken chosen to be

even before he left led a '55 Blue Note date
of March 29th *Afro-Cuban* his then ten-inch
with his three fine originals seemed a cinch
to make it as a leader his trumpet solo great

on his "Minor's Holiday" Grieg's "Anitra's
Dance" lifting him to new daring new drive
Potato's conga elevates too & if "Afrodisia"
a letdown "Basheer's Dream" comes alive

K on top Cecil's baritone touching bottom
with Mobe's reed tasting of a cigar & rum
J.J.'s trombone a smooth full-bodied break
as Art Horace bass Pettiford shake & bake

on Kenny's warm dreamy "Lotus Flower"
Silver to enervate all with his piano intro
& soon its Homeric fruit makes J.J. blow
an indolent Odysseus in his funky bower

earlier on January 30th had cut three sides
Hank Cecil Horace & Art same as March
but Percy on bass as KD on his cab rides
jotting "Echo of Spring" for New York's

wintry skies staved hopeful quarter notes
tires spinning on ice as his melody floats
on lines read Every Good Boy Does Fine
in F-A-C-E spaces sharp flat natural sign

later in a Jersey studio Rudy laying down
"K.D.'s Motion" "La Villa" & "Venita's
Dance" his trumpet work solid but found
Lion deciding to hold up the set's release

even with Hank & Cecil in superior form
with Percy's bass wonderful in tune-after-
tune & Horace-Art underpinnings as ever
only in '87 to issue K playing up a storm

in two February '56 volumes KD on tour
with the Birdland Stars of Al Cohn tenor
Phil Woods' alto Conte Candoli trumpet
Ernie Wilkins' lucky charts of "Roulette"

& "Minorin' the Blues" & out of the pen
of Manny Albam his "Two Pairs of Aces"
paying off on the KD-Conte 4-bar chases
a black & a white as if one another's twin

suits differ tonal quality a matching hand
mixing spade with heart club or diamond
as two together a deck-high numbered set
trumps any four face cards full or straight

spot in stanza above terms loaded as dice
a risk taken as rightly race & gender raise
resentful looks if a word rolls snake eyes
unintended sense explodes & writer pays

but a chance worth taking no crap-game
bet placed on the dozen pips of numbers
on a die up side win or lose it encumbers
unlike letters in a real or figurative name

hitting memory's jackpot with Dameron
whose *Fontainebleau* would cut in NYC
March 9th '56 a sextet Payne on the bary
again & Coker on 'bone Shadow Wilson

drums John Simmons bass Sahib on alto
Joe Alexander tenor with Tadd on piano
his sound impressions of palace gardens
lakes swans forests summon Napoleon's

L'Adieu of another March his 1814 exile
as fountains invaded dreams on Elba isle
a hallucinating not "Delirium" of Tadd's
his frenzied joy no New Orleanian trad's

first chorus Joe's his with rollicking licks
then Gitler's "crackling" Ken as he kicks
the proceedings into literally higher gear
satisfying with lyrical runs clean & clear

KD never again with Joe from Cleveland
a rejoicing tenor but April 4th teams with
J.R. for tick-tocking tongue-attack frolics
turn on a dime a river's flow roiling sand

together on Chessmates label as The Jazz
Prophets with Sam Jones' bass Dick Katz
piano Arthur Edgehill drums on title tune
K's "The Prophet" that tenor man a boon

to omens seer-leader'd read in minor key
portending close-knit unit's future venue
a Café Bohemia booking tapings by Blue
Note same as when had been with Blakey

but now his wings spread as never before
& if blind to pecking with Monterose will
end so soon yet shows has begun to fulfill
his early signs as soothsayer reading soar-

ing bird in an upper region unexplored by
even the epic poets as he works its swing-
ingly happy theme with élan & not letting
up until with his cadenza he says bye-bye

each sideman strong in his way bold solo-
ing by Sam on K's "Blues Elegante" & by
Dick comping till tenorist enters all aglow
to carry the torch passed to K holds it high

his "DX" as good as it gets as fast & fluid
he & J.R. each on a veritable changes tear
unriddling "I Got Rhythm" as if any druid
augurs by blood gushing from bull or hare

chord progressions in a mysterious tongue
of brass & reed with the fingers & thumbs
hammering keys skins or strings as moon-
driven as tides percussing at night or noon

religio-pulsation seasonal as sap from root
to leaf & bud a groove sacred to all wilting
or faint of heart no Inquisition with execut-
ing of heretics or a Quijote windmill tilting

as if a benediction Billie's "Don't Explain"
lyricsless version Dick & muted K convert
to notes of a parable expresses love & pain
the hushed acceptance of happiness & hurt

session ends with K's 6/8 "Tahitian Suite"
becomes "Monaco" at the Blue Note date
of May 31 when only Katz to be replaced
by Bobby Timmons then 19 just a 2-week

rehearsal with the unit plus Kenny Burrell
on guitar not on their alternate take of this
renamed tune while K on May 22nd Signal
session with Cecil Payne doing again Diz'

"Groovin' High" better on "Saucer Eyes"
a relaxing Randy Weston theme although
at times it seems K can't get started relies
on licks from Grieg & Grofé a faulty solo

in "Bringing Up Father" "Man of Moods"
too did he miss J.R.'s tenor a minor blues
could have since with his own "Monaco"
at Café Bohemia both the horns really go

after Bob & K in an easygoing Latin beat
K changing to his intensely driving swing
a double-timing but no melodramatic feat
as Feather observes K's eighth-note string

of lines broken by graces & syncopations
but all with a mood J.R.'s tenor maintains
by hard attacks end in gentler fluent turns
lion to lambkin his lesson a listener learns

"'Round About Midnight" a Monk classic
& on it KD J.R. & Bob just as good if not
better than Thelonious himself with K hot
& high but ice-age cool as after a Jurassic

& following test of mind & soul K's own
theme titled for the place earlier dreamed
would visit seeds of "Mexico City" sown
as plowed planted hoed churned creamed

no Hernán Cortés a conquistador foretold
in the codices as a destined ruler of fertile
fields as Montezuma'd known for a while
to come from sunrise to receive with gold

then damned Uichilobos & the other gods
forbid offerings of sacrificial virgin hearts
crosses no bloody altars so rebellion starts
the avaricious drowned as against all odds

others battle to escape on causeways drop
their riches in saving lives a Botello warn-
ing leave or not to survive a night of horn
& whistle calls for combat-harvested crop

& would heed their own true necromancer
when Trojans ignored Cassandra's answer
to a lying Sinon & believed too in the sign
for Narvaez defeat pig with navel on spine

like a lady at Central Market danced alone
to Lost & Nameless Ork & Eric Hokkanen
a Finn with bass electric guitar & his violin
regretted her breasts sagged to belly button

did K read Bernal Díaz del Castillo's vivid
account or of the Aztec auspice lifted a lid
on future tribes would recognize this locus
by snake in the eagle's beak atop of cactus

to spot it on Lake Texcoco's marshy island
or hear paired trumpets in a mariachi band
or Copland's dance-hall *El Salón* bare feet
in that "hot spot" lent Aaron a primal beat

perhaps absorbed it through blues osmosis
as Ken's "Sunrise in Mexico" even echoes
Cortés's coming whereas "City" proves its
"exotic boppish flavor" may be "grooviest

item in exciting session" Feather says with
soloists up to K's setting a precipitate pace
his impetuous break declares he's ever kith
& kin with sounds of any age & every race

a gait sustained by J.R.'s turbine of a tenor
its whirls twists & turns assertive or tender
peaceful war counts no casualties as guitar
& piano disarm till K reprises the final bar

from a newer Spain to "A Night in Tunisia"
Dizzy's take on the Sahara's North African
dunes with KD's notes as if of a dust-laden
simoon prelude to storm blown out of Asia

J.R. picking up on Rousseau negress asleep
her mandolin struck chords in Picasso et al
lion had caught her scent yet to let her keep
her desert life with tenor man playing it all

then K to announce "Autumn in New York"
his eloquence evoking Duke's lyrics mingle
new-love pain & longing for a far-off castle
the darkness blessing slums & Central Park

then his & Klook's "Royal Roost" as KD's
puissant rightful proof of his co-authorship
over Rollins's "Tenor Madness" Mobley's
"Sportin' Crowd" & then to slow their clip

on Rodgers & Hart's "My Heart Stood Still"
from no ritual knife but just one look at her
as leader states the theme of that optic thrill
& solos in even eighths as a melodic master

yet mastery can't assure survival much less
control not even success of a storied Cortés
he forced to retreat with Tlaxcaltecan allies
barbarians providing food & water supplies

& K despite the omens auspices & auguries
disbanded a standout unit gave up unable to
wrangle sufficient work & the pathetic Blue
Note royalties not even covering union fees

yet would not give up entirely on leadership
just withdrawing as Hernán also MacArthur
two came back a shrewd determined lawyer
invading in ships Douglas his stiff upper lip

& "I Shall Return" K in his own good time
his name as the headliner on album sleeves
meanwhile joining others to place the lime-
light on their record dates ring laurel leaves

on June 15th K paired with fellow trumpeter
Donald Byrd in Phil Woods' Septet Prestige
studio gig as of December Don a newcomer
took the Messengers seat now he Art's liege

the future solo star in wide demand but here
his choruses lacking continuity get hung up
in 8- or 4-bar chases where the veteran's ear
knows whither it goes gets there with no rup-

tured rhythm repeated vapid fatuous pattern
mostly on "Pairing Off" with Ken's unusual
figures filling his break inspires Phil in turn
to his best showcase as too from Don's final

phrase Gene Quill takes his finest alto flight
then on "Suddenly It's Spring" the trumpets
embrace its tune with Donald to hug it tight
in bits & pieces K kisses it nearly breathless

each complementing other in hard-bop style
if their gift of gab not to say it all whose has
Satch's in a way & Bird's did too for a while
K's a lesser yet prophetic of increasing class

before after between free-lanced with friends
July 19 with Gee again as part of his all-stars
septet date to exhibit Matt but still it depends
on sidemen will make the most of fewer bars

to bring out best in tunes its leader's originals
a namesaked "Gee!" & a "Kingston Lounge"
"The Boys From Brooklyn" though GM hails
from Houston bayous unlike his lively sounds

on July 27th K joins Messengers stablemates
for Mobley's *Second Message* Doug Watkins
Blakey & Silver all together again with Ken's
smoky tone (Ira Gitler phrase) communicates

Hank's latinized "Message From the Border"
its then bargain boots & booze today disorder
gruesome drug wars of Montezuma's revenge
but hear in mellow trumpet & tenor no binge

of decapitation just feel their "I Should Care"
Cahn ballad with Ken pouring out a heartfelt
reading hurts to listen as he & the tenor melt
an inner berg as if emissions warming the air

as answer to "Who Cares" Gershwin's lyrics
declare love matters is unconcerned firms go
under blue chips fall a feeling K would know
had cut Ira's song with his Prophets May '56

he pianist & guitarist take cuteness in stride
all the crew as well on Harris's "Crazeology"
in letting rip if tenorist squeaks K's dizzy ride
boggles mind with its sonic speed & accuracy

& just not into strings of notes to show it on
Mobe's easy-going "Xlento" with K opening
at its medium tempo with his swing flows on
& on an effortless thinking is simply singing

in August K recording again "I Should Care"
now on his friend Ernie Henry's debut album
the men had long before this worked together
in a Brooklyn basement practicing in tandem

perfecting brass & reed playing as if one man
by the blending as a pair enriching each other
on the ballad the horns no catch-as-catch-can
but taking turns as tones lead into one another

as Ovid's red-hair Ocyrhoe's tale runs quickly
from Aesculapius' motherless birth to her say-
ing his cures will bear power to heal the sickly
till gods check her chants & stop her prophecy

brings to mind blues in Ernie's "Cleo's Chant"
where he & KD tell it like it is & shall ever be
since in every age someone will always resent
gifts of speech & medicine or a music artistry

as something there is cuts short an Ernie's life
at 31 & Clifford Brown's even earlier only 25
who had they lived as long as the others alive
a decade later both then would have been rife

with awards have surely achieved even more
reached to higher rungs up the ladder of jazz
yet what Who's Who's to say for sure or has
a predictive vision to see past futurity's door

had Kenny died before he took Miles's place
with Bird or would take over Clifford's chair
with Max & encyclopedia devoted less space
to reporting his briefer career would any care

even when Roach would pick him as the one
to replace the irreplaceable heir to the throne
all bemoaned an apparent king with so much
promise barely listened to KD's Midas touch

Replacing a Remembered Great

few dare even attempt it since better
or equal rare as conquistador admits
an aboriginal glue & copper helmets
superior to Spain's & *he*'s the debtor

oftener can't hack it as plastics break
when stainless steel can last for years
& as for Progress in art for art's sake
some saying there is none only peers

with literature Homer & Shakespeare
in jazz can number Kenny & Clifford
& yet for some KD was nowhere near
to ebullient Brownie who ever soared

but then Ken drives "a row of sabers"
wrote *Harmony Illustrated* of his own
airborne line slices dices never wavers
& also melodious as any aria's known

maybe the comparisons come to little
& yet are made in hopes they'll settle
partisan quarrels though when do they
ever perhaps'll aid if hoping to weigh

what/who's best to listen to for & why
compare-contrast if only self to satisfy
not to take anything from the younger
but requite the elder a debt of wonder

& so begin with June 18th of '56 eight
days before "the greatest new trumpet"
would slide in his car off that rain-wet
artery & bequeath a legacy few create

on that final concert Max called "Just
One of Those Things" love not death
on Clifford's mind but most with lust
on theirs joints drinks on their breath

while that model life of Brown made
its sudden end more tragic still along
with the loss of his instrument's song
its "Joy Spring" he inimitably played

his "fabulous flights" in Cole Porter's
lyrical phrase but also his "too hot not
to cool down" a cosmic fact all forgot
in hearing Brownie's stirring quarters

his exuberant eighth & sixteenth notes
even though the most admiring of ears
may tire of a synaptosomal firing sears
the nerves or pinches impulse & bloats

the sorrowful case at that Norfolk club
as Clifford went until if he wasn't blue
sober listeners may've turned that hue
& fled the smoke & its satanic hubbub

with pointless pandemonic runs so fast
& far too many to mean any more than
mere technique & if Kenny on that last
Messengers date took it at a same fran-

tic tempo & would shortly take it again
for *Max + 4* on September 17th yet Ken
by then at ease with any speed his brain
in control as cheeks puffed with oxygen

trained along with glossal & diaphragm
refrain from overbearing of lips & teeth
varying velocity as if in retiming a cam
to slower grooves over quicker beneath

though each decelerated & both applied
their brakes to Haggart's "What's New"
with its solo Butterfield originally blew
KD & Brownie's renditions day & night

the latter's surely a bravura performance
supremacy displayed in his June farewell
while KD in '59 to dig deeper in the mel-
ody's vein mining from it a rich advance

even on October 10 '56 on "I Get a Kick
Out of You" K's opening chorus stupen-
dous flawless & far more fetching driven
by Max's slashing cymbals with his stick

his thundering bass drum a rattling snare
to K's darting & dashing as never before
while on the Porter tune Brown was rare-
ly so off & sadly soon he'd play no more

on the 30th Oliver Nelson & Ken to meet
for a Prestige/New Jazz session the tenor-
ist too to go too soon yet death no winner
since both horns handed it a sound defeat

each to take a turn to answer the question
posed in title of ballad by Bobcats bassist
whose chords KD probes as a metallurgist
testing for valence in titanium or tungsten

his solo a poignant self-responsive Q & A
as with one moving phrase he interrogates
& with his next replies till it in turn awaits
coming of query & a cadenza's tender say

& true of Brownie's improvisation in '53
on "Hymn of the Orient" for his *New Star
on the Horizon* leader album features Gigi
Gryce's alto & that tune of his in its minor

key inquired by Clifford's quizzical mind
inspecting its theme investigating its tonic
looking through the relative major to find
consonance dissonance parallel harmonic

as in delving into dominant & other keys
to discover in these his echoic comeback
to his own inquisition of each tonal series
his profuse vigor seemed he'd never lack

in not three years blotted out though hear
it still on a Blue Note *best of disc* & four-
&-a-half after the fatal crash K to appear
doing Gigi's tune Brownie'd done before

but in this case KD's can't match B's solo
missing Clifford's fire never coming alive
never working usual logical magical drive
& rest of Golson's Sextet just barely so-so

with exception of the J.J. trombone break
though Johnson had topped himself in '53
when he & Brownie recorded "Get Happy"
with Heath bros Clarke Lewis wide awake

June 22 that was & the trumpeteer a force
to be reckoned with his horn-sound strong
as the proverbial bull or the real one gores
the toreador & then again K tagging along

to face on October 31 the Birdland crowd
on Arlen's tune but the bass's over-miked
making K too faint Gene Ramey too loud
yet pumps up KD so he's clearly psyched

on entering like gangbusters quoting from
"When the Red Red Robin" & bebopping
till Art Blakey butts in & ruins everything
ending the happiness with too much drum

if sacrilege even of Max the same be said
for on their last concert in '56 Roach took
over to hog "Daahoud" the Brownie cook-
er though Clifford's soloing but a retread

& not even so good though articulate still
straining for high notes senseless & shrill
fallen off from his earliest reading of '54
first recorded with Pacific Jazz's rapport

of sidemen in a studio premiering Brown
letting loose his lion roar as if an MGM's
Shelly's short & tasteful fills a Zoot Sims
unfancy tenor every white eager to crown

him Emperor Jones Stu's valve trombone
Russ's piano Joe's bass & Bob's baritone
all jumping together in playing tribute to
their princely primate with no hullabaloo

& on December 12th from Café Bohemia
through a live radio cast Max & his Four
paying homage to their adored bete noire
doing his "Daahoud" but it's like anemia

with its tempo slower & KD not quite up
to his surer-lipped solo on "I Feel a Song
Coming On" where Ken & Sonny's erup-
tions on imperial winds copy King Kong

beating his chest above the Empire State
while the snatch of "Bye Bye Blackbird"
in the tenor's boisterous chorus unheard
in "I Feel" from Brown's May 22nd date

as once more B's preceded KD's version
though Clifford's showing no real uptick
in his acumen but just protean technique
as more time no guarantee won't worsen

yet given longer Ken'll continue to grow
& let not CB's lovelier tone overshadow
K's black-widow weft of dewdrop gems
sparkling in light of maturer stratagems

as when in March of '57 on "Valse Hot"
his horn's in perfect unanimity with Son-
ny's tenor the two in three as if were one
& after Rollins rocks K throws to a spot

with his release smooth as pitcher tosses
a knuckle-curve Ken's a Woody hollow-
tree cartoon strike & by mixing staccato
& legato recorded more wins than losses

CB too though on same May 22nd session
will fluff at times Rollins' waltzing theme
a thing Ken rarely ever did with any team
yet Clifford scores with his note selection

neither clears the fence in "I'll Remember
April" their chases with tenor mostly bore
though the DePaul line Brown does render
with a gorgeous tone while K returns more

to touch base often with a thematic phrase
relating his exercise-like figures & impart-
ing to their conscious stream his "rip-snort-
ing" ride no tiresome scales Brownie plays

if Ken's ending cleverly alters the tune still
his outing of May '57 & Brown's from '56
aren't among their best nor is the memorial
KD sings to the "uncrowned king" in lyrics

Jon Hendricks wrote for Golson's threnody
"I Remember Clifford" but more important
is Ken's feeling for his fellow *rey* one can't
help but hear in his vocal's verse & melody

& all K says of Brown in his *Sings & Plays*
of August '58 can say of him seems always
near with a sound some have tried to repeat
yet cannot take his place nor quite compete

with one so uniquely real his "smoky" tone
his alone & did not nor thought to dethrone
the regal confrere as none becomes another
yet put himself in felt the shoes of a brother

Maxing & More

does growing come of forming a part
gain proceed from giving in up away
is adding to enlarging or loss of heart
of self or ego one or group go or stay

for the rest of '56 with Max & Sonny
on October 5th Wade Legge on piano
now along with bass George Morrow
in tribute to Charlie playing a medley

a selection picked by tenor as session
leader from pieces the Yard recorded
& with each tune the soloist afforded
a chance for showing his stuff as Son

does first when on "I Remember You"
heralds with "Parker's Mood" & then
mellows honks & rips an homage due
to the bebop genius & afterwards Ken

on "My Melancholy Baby" to stumble
outa the gate but rapidly to recover his
equilibrium & then again he'll fumble
as tries to vary his tonguing & phrases

yet bends with affective force & works
the chords for all they're worth but run-
ning them here more as a derby for fun
than to defeat the field & take its purse

then on "Just Friends" comes off better
in combining choices of touching notes
with dazzling lines the Bird & Ken ver-
sions both can stir but Charlie's emotes

a loftier majestic flight on eagle's wings
lifted by Jimmy Carroll's harp & strings
Stan Freeman's keys Mitch Miller oboe
Ray Brown-Buddy Rich rhythm combo

as the altoist swoops down with soulful
sound & a luscious virtuosity nonpareil
master class from '49 intricate & equal-
ly playful an aerie of *such* ideas & style

& next the Quintet offering "Star Eyes"
a theme shared by the horns then tenor
alone after Ken had opened with more
of a laidback mode less so in improvis-

ing yet still relaxed with melodic turns
& a double-up burst impeccably kerns
as the founder lettering a metallic face
for printed page Ken for singing grace

in '51 neither Miles nor Bird so perfect
the latter less than his monumental self
yet still at moments not a dwarf nor elf
as he leaps pitch distances few connect

tunes his stellar ear to undulating astral
waves while Miles with light pixy tone
he'd never hide under a bushel or stone
exposes in its changes his new & subtle

his nuanced seductive approach to song
not one K to take himself & yet his own
entices too by a sincerity he if not alone
expressed from the get-go & right along

in '57 pictured twice for *Jazz Contrasts*
as the album's leader its supporting cast
Max & Sonny pianist Hank Jones Oscar
Pettiford bass plus Betty Glamman harp

she not on "Falling in Love With Love"
where Ken's candor lies in the clarity of
his straight-ahead funky staccato tongue
trustworthy & not fooling around as Son-

ny's does though the tenor's witty asides
& his surprising turnback tones entertain
& teach bop's loving lesson none derides
when learned it from his amorous refrain

on "Larue" a ballad Brownie had written
& named for his wife but never recorded
Gigi Gryce's arrangement has harp begin
one of man's oldest instruments reported

dates from ca. 3000 B.C. in Mesopotamia
crescent of contrasts desert to salty marsh
cradle of civil literate cities but also harsh
religious law a swift river bordering Syria

its Tigris of KD's running style Euphrates
of his leisurely pace their confluence near
the port of Basra on Shatt-al-Arab Betty's
classical & Kenny's jazz each other's peer

polarities flowing together with her thumb
plucking string thrumming glissando scale
as his fingers & lips hit high or low to nail
the warmest tone a stirring trickier rhythm

after the faultless K cadenza on "My Old
Flame" harpist finishing with a poignant
ring to her pedaled chord & with K hold-
ing final "But Beautiful" note to her hint

of sentiment spices up K's unsaccharine
sound if not the androgynous intonation
of breathy Chet K's too a wistful timbre
breaks a heart or makes it gayly somber

then Ken's "La Villa" in double-up time
the tenor adding a soulful tone to its rich
harmonic writing & KD in his solo licks
hits with killer-dillers but these no crime

Sonny & Hank too into a shooting spree
as Max fires off his fitting tuned percus-
sive caps till K will end the friendly fuss
by blasting one last round of his melody

a question now has come & it has before
why go on disc by disc could skip ignore
or forget instead of a listing date by date
what is the point just to repeat how great

not quite nor simply to celebrate defend
or congratulate though these too all legit
even if having once begun must finish it
still the music between beginning & end

each collegial meeting bruits a meaning
furnishes the means can make these tick
each distinct each like the kindling stick
or the spark for igniting of a kerosening

emblazons simile's imagery on catching
fire from his flame or his white-hot coal
a faster heat or slower warmth matching
those of fellow *músicos* & if takes a toll

with few if any readers making it to here
with patience maxed out as a credit card
used beyond its rates bankrupter offered
will risk it all go for broke write off fear

so back to Ken is now with "The Mobe"
for his August 18 *Curtain Call* KD him-
self yet not the same as the gyring globe
alters on spinning facets of a single gem

best of all elongated shafts a few slightly
bent refract on passing into a lake or sea
the "Rêverie" of Debussy a tune Clinton
arranged added to its title "My" the own-

ership any's enters its shimmering dream
yet Kenton's version neither/nor not jazz
nor delicate poetic classical liquid stream
if Rollins' May '56 inspired doesn't daz-

zle as K's splendorous scintillating does
at faster tempo than saxophone colossus
yet never rushes even if he double-times
to render his subtler atmospheric rhymes

never a chime or jingle too close together
tonal echoing never jars for farther afield
than Hank's tenor from melodic measure
& surely K's liberties would've appealed

to that Frenchman recommended indirect
caresses of piano keys & touch of fingers
softly firm impressionistic meistersingers
Claude & Ken not averse to rubato effect

"Don't Get Too Hip" Mobe's own advice
yet in Ansell's book Hank & KD ultra-hip
with K on this bluesy tune funky by twice
with licks may allude to "One Mint Julep"

if hot not lewd nor sexy in degraded ways
on "Curtain Call" speeding a happy chase
on "The Mobe" too & then "My Reverie"
M "On the Bright Side" to end it joyously

& now with Ernie Henry Ken has started
a partnership sadly to last so short a time
like Fats & Brownie Henry good-hearted
as they he if older at 31 gone in his prime

a roll call so long of those at an early age
left the scene had more to say maybe not
Bird at 35 a "has-been" hard bop the rage
long live his sidemen! the Kingpin's shot

even among the letter B any list includes
Bix Bubber & Bunny with the first at 28
next two 29 & 33 first & last from booze
though on Columbia & Victor still create

six weeks before his high blood pressure
did Ernie in & just three prior to the end
Riverside recorded the enduring treasure
of K's own quartet on *2 horns//2 rhythm*

a trove from exotica & warhorse to blues
ballad novelty & a number KD baroques
to take on all but "Soon" a new approach
with no piano chords to restrict or choose

as Gerry Mulligan & Jimmy Giuffre had
a greater freedom for his & Ernie's "strol-
ling" Orrin's word & if sort of then a fad
K as into inert clay breathes a living soul

"Lotus Blossom"'s first but November 13
'59 two years to the day K'd cut a version
far mellower fuller than this though G.T.'s
drumming keeps all alert to save the piece

from any listener's hasty urge to deprecate
K's stretching out letting go as too abstract
a word Roach had used to describe the fact
K tends to hover above earth's love & hate

reaches for a kind of Pollack-Rothko plane
beyond a reclining nude a mushroom cloud
removed from yet aware of madding crowd
K unlike painters undriven by suicidal pain

the same drove a Plath Sexton & Berryman
K if tangled in notes or tied up like Houdini
in "Is It True What They Say About Dixie?"
or "The End of the Affair" somehow to man-

age his extrication from every chordal chain
straitjacket a sunken vault & again to aspire
to art's high calling for as Miles'd maintain
just K & Dizzy's horns could to him inspire

at the piano K to open "Soon" with a Monk-
ish arpeggiated run his trumpet with Ernie's
alto in exact accord as two extend or release
bass bowing & walking with plaintive plunk

so moving to hear Ernie's intensely keening
singing of the Gershwin tune among his last
sung above dirge of K's keyboard mourning
as if sensing this friend soon to have passed

& knew wouldn't be saying "I'll Be Seeing
You" for after this life believed in no other
but could share the song before his leaving
as a couple in war parted from one another

Ken seeming to return in his farewell tone
the mates of '41 to '45 had not come back
his buzzing low-register bittersweet attack
recalling battlefield moon's one face alone

with Ernie at his most emotionally charged
restoring the courtship's old familiar places
lyrics hummed on waiting to be discharged
his alto obbligato to the theme KD retraces

& on his "Noose Bloos" with its bluesy feel
K lets loose with astringent high tight shake
his final phrase picked up by Henry to make
a solo of his own beautifully touchingly real

& if none of this were enough "Jazz-Classic"
last but not least K's piece with angular leap
announces its blending of the harmony basic
to fugal Bach with a beat can't help but keep

but then remembering "this world . . . in tune"
Ira's words to George & his haunting "Soon"
still casts on the recording a heavy tragic pall
for with altoist gone the album turns funereal

though after loss KD as others would carry on
his load lightened on again entering the studio
to record with Max Mobe & bass but no piano
as his Quartet did but this for a Bird had flown

doing his compositions from "Parker's Mood"
to "KoKo" "Yardbird Suite" & one with Dizzy
Chazz cooked up their classic "Anthropology"
& too a Cleanhead "Tune-Up" with an attitude

but "Confirmation" can do as just one tune KD
blew with Bird at Royal Roost on February 19
of '49 with Max Al & Tommy all on the scene
to back them up as the section had so regularly

after frontline's played its theme K with mute
Bird coming with mind-blowing all-out attack
& then Ken's open with his more singing tack
his "pretty phrase" Al picks up & follows suit

Max to drum a deep-toned break more appeal-
ing than his long solo taken on Morrow Mobe
KD & his December 23 '57 set when K to reel
off lines illuminating as Bird's flashing strobe

then Hank & Ken trilling on ascending a chromatic scale as K would again April 21st of '64
then with Harris piano Euell bass a Heath bro
Albert "Tootie" drums the Bird tune as before

& even while HARYOU private tape distorts
KD's sound confirms its growth loud & clear
& on his announcing the selections even hear
his boyish voice eager as any roots for sports

in Harris's solo ideas come if not furious fast
as Bird's & like his with such a terrific swing
then Ken to trade bars with Tootie who's last
in line & on skins & cymbals to rattle & ping

on May 26 of '68 on nearing Ken's final year
he'd be recorded to do Bird's tune as a tribute
to Fats Brownie & Booker Little the last mute
at 23 all too early each a cherished trumpeteer

joined with five others played the instrument
among them at a Jamaica Queens Club Ruby
Galveston native Richard Williams had spent
time with Mingus band Bill Hardman Woody

Shaw & Blue Mitchell but on "Confirmation"
just together with Bill & Richard as K to solo
first with his flurry of notes in a melodic flow
many surprise some intense or downright fun

& each at the core warmer than the hard edge
of Hardman's biting tones with most a pledge
of allegiance to Brownie's own yet even then
his chorus a superb memorial to all three men

powerhouse Richard the roundhouse mop-up
starts high & reaches higher to pack a wallop
seems at times to run out of steam but not for
long as he bounces back up from off the floor

not one's knocked out by either of the others
just jabbing & jawing & blowing as brothers
at their "trumpet summit" each musician pay-
ing respects to the music had heard them play

with Max & Mobe again on January 14th '58
to cut six tunes include Max's "Audio Blues"
"That Ole Devil Love" K's own "Speculate"
& Hank's "C.M." where KD's light & loose

& Ramsey Lewis too his piano the delightful
addition to a laidback session with the excep-
tion of Ken's runaway piece unmeant to mull
with trumpet tenor & pianist each full of pep

in July-August K to fulfill a long-held dream
of having a recording of vocals he could sing
a thing he'd done himself in Gillespie's band
& later from taking voice lessons had trained

his phrasing & breath control for had always
memorized the lyrics of songs helps had said
in relating of words to all the tones one plays
increases meaning of notes had heard or read

on "Autumn Leaves" enunciating each sylla-
ble pellucidly unadorned with barely vibrato
other than the brief quaver at the end to fill a
line but in his vocal not any trumpet staccato

behind him Curtis Fuller on muted trombone
K's high voice almost deepened to a baritone
& then on his own muted horn adds a further
dimension to this song with words of Mercer

if not a chance his singing could replace his
trumpet playing as Nat Cole's did his piano
& if a little beyond his range on "From This
Moment On" can articulate the lyrics know-

ingly on "Angel Eyes" his timing fine a nice
contrasting chorus on horn & handles higher
notes of his closing vocal line with a surpris-
ing aplomb after the shortcomings of a prior

attempt but K not one for giving up growing
stronger as he goes along for his delivery on
"Where Are You" K's most piquant showing
with a more lovely muted trumpet-trombone

then come October 13th he's on *Stereo Drive*
the fed-on-classical-discord Cecil Taylor title
changed to *Coltrane Time* with its label alive
to market share the PR department never idle

& yet K's "Shifting Down" & Chuck Israels'
"Double Clutching" go better with original's
mixed car & phono metaphor if not the same
be said for blues with Schönbergian pianism

even so KD can hear Cecil's frontier chords
blockhouse or the pup tent flapping in wind
& sounds at ease firing away as if to defend
to hold the fort against the dissonant hordes

not only versatile but a respectable scouting
a getting the lay of its land native/European
& then on "Just Friends" his aim to recover
its theme if C swings horse of another color

the tenor unmistakable on K's opening tune
but with the piano's tones two giants collide
whether new or old Ken takes it all in stride
ever adapting unwrapped in a same cocoon

Blue Train more himself on "Like Someone
in Love" & Kenny too while Cecil can clash
& near derail but engines on without a crash
bassist keeping all on track till takes're done

nothing here of the tenorist's sheeted sound
soprano "pure emotion" over modal ground
none of pianist's "naked fire" "protoplasm"
ballistics of balletic leaps at highest volume

if 'Trane & Taylor's album no John sublime
nor a glimpse of the smashing Cecil to come
sneak previews undaunted K soon to appear
an emergent imago in his breakthrough year

Arriving

out of the chrysalis of bop & hard bop
K tries his wings in a '59 lower-keyed
Riverside flight with *Blue Spring* drop-
ping the temperature reducing the heat

to a balmy April day as he & Adderley
slow it down with less of Cannonball's
grandstanding sax & in his scoring KD
offers lusher lines his solo rises & falls

in "Spring Is Here" not above the staff
more often into earthier tones as tubers
root in a compost heap & as purple saf-
fron flowers from mold the cucumbers

watermelon sweet as bee pollen basket
keeps the cycle alive Ken's own septet
doing the same but minus pyrotechnics
just tendril-quick runs in his "Poetic"'s

tender strain as David Amram's French
horn warms up chords & Cecil's lyrical
baritone booms lighter with Cannonball
rushing before then letting go a drench-

ing rain of reedy notes a feeding of ears
with his kernels of gold nourish beyond
the metal itself a richer growth no pond
whose view to bream crop-duster blears

by a chemical spray on one-time stream
pristine as his alto flows onward after K
came first with both testing the extreme
limits of the wind instruments they play

& though they've gone still blowing yet
through electric outlet amplifier speaker
set-up of mid-range with bass & tweeter
each's breeze a greening fruit-giving jet

Cedar Walton's piano at times Brubeck-
ian for like their leader a versatile Texan
Adderley at his best on "Spring Cannon"
K named for him on chases neck & neck

was it at this session he'd hear the altoist
yodel *la-d-odle la-d-odle* as he said he'd
heard the Bird before but first farm folks
with the sacks of bolls pulled & weighed

on the range a lone cowboy at end of day
then back at the corral uncinching saddle
yet unlike the sax his horn unable to play
ye-o-dle la-de ye-o-dle of cotton & cattle

on his "Passion Spring" he & A hand-in-
glove with K in soloing down low again
yet more exploratory a Tayor's influence
could be with Cannonball deeply intense

& on "It Might As Well Be Spring" feel-
ing Rodgers' gay-melancholy lover tune
so truly K sets his indelible staccato seal
on fever season has never come too soon

in '58 Ken would don his teaching gown
on August 29 '59 his class going to town
in Lenox School's Berkshire music barn
woods & hills once home to Hawthorne

& Melville too when he wrote his epical
prose & did K know of Herman's whale
or of humpbacked "inveterate composer
of song" a sounding cetacean as exposer

of danger above or with it a call for love
these he knew & taught to students from
Pete Farmer to the famed Don Cherry of
his/Ornette's *The Shape of Jazz to Come*

Ken saying of the Lenox mentor system
wished when came to NYC there'd been
such one-to-one instruction to show him
the ropes would have begged to be let in

of Ken's October 26 live Randy Weston
Five Spot session the less said the better
to a blue Monday add its dreary weather
its charts by a hospitalized Melba Liston

no time to run through a "High Fly" first
as Hawk & Roy Haynes's flights delayed
great tenor just warming up yet had paid
his dues could do that piece unrehearsed

together with K's horn a gorgeous sound
the two producing but soloing over stop-
time piano chords even KD's heard pop-
ping clams when he too had been around

for before & after Ken's hooking up with
Bean another Coleman Hawkins moniker
out of a long '23 to then legendary career
the trumpeter a mainstay of saxophonists

of whichever persuasion from Swing-age
florid romantic to the Bird's cerebral bop
or the raucous soulful roar 'Trane so pop-
ularized with copycats taking up his gage

can count some three-dozen reed men K
had recorded with & wonder what other
trumpet to engage so many from Mobley
Moody Rollins Monterose Heath brother

Jim to Land McLean Dolphy Henderson
leaves out those like Henry lesser known
but K paired with any gave each his best
assisted all to shine on east coast or west

Oliver Nelson had never met when studio
called KD to come in for the October 30th
quintet date with tenor from St. Louie Mo
had "been through the big band mill" with

units like the Nat Towles & Louie Bellson
always sitting in an alto chair till switched
to his larger axe but yet his higher weapon
heard cutting lyrically as his lower pitched

taking the edge off the bigger's harder bite
& making it into Jack Maher's softer quite
gentler carver his "salty dog" as on Ollie's
opener his own original "Jams and Jellies"

where KD plays his "pin wheels of sound"
needing the bread but ready to lend a hand
dependable in any supporting roles as here
he sustains "Passion Flower" "atmosphere

of [Billy Strayhorn] impressionism" while
tenor mixes slow & fast with "reverential"
in this ballad's "real" Ellingtonian "voice"
& with K muted the due respectful choice

then open on "Don't Stand Up" K's bright
happy tone perfectly matching Ollie's own
a rendering of his original theme o so right
& his break few tenors have ever outshone

O's "Ostinato" a fuller showcase for a KD
solo filled with an authoritative coming on
yet is equaled & even yes outdone by Ollie
pours it on with his quoting & snappy tone

as for "What's New" could say some more
but have gone into its loveliness heretofore
so add on "Booze Blues Baby" all at home
on this funky closing tune O's as if shalom

on November 13 it's *Quiet Kenny*'s arrival
as on this album with only his horn accom-
panied by piano bass & drums Ken's trum-
pet now to measure up in no sense of rival-

ry with any had proven their worth before
but brings to bear on a song a predecessor
had left his stamp upon a KD new-minted
responsive mood not a reading reinvented

the case with "My Ideal" a tune the Hawk
had cut in '43 & K had heard with "Body
& Soul" from '39 the tenor's peerless talk
via fifths tonic bridge a smidge of melody

but on that later piece Ken the one's more
moving with muted tones more than stack
up with a Bean's lush rhapsodic runs lack-
ing in K's restraint his passion never over-

done but with one deep-felt poignant note
his a voluminous speech as too a selective
Flanagan piano tone or a full chord of five
fingers can touch & leave a catch in throat

on his own "Blue Friday" K low & bluesy
an open horn altered as if muted or maybe
with a hand in bell his varied sound a case-
book blues prescriptive of phase or phrase

lovely the only word for Kenny on "Alone
Together" a tune for Maher closer to home
since K recalled his first doing it with Bird
here drops so low hits a rock-bottom nerve

with "I Had the Craziest Dream" Ken join-
ing the ranks of voices exceptional even in
a music as unique as American jazz whose
tongue speaks instant sense in pop or blues

bending his notes for their delicious blend-
ing of happy & hurt now making his mark
but not as Harry James in '42 had depend-
ed more on soaring high as morning's lark

K rather digging deeper into emotive veins
exploring the subterranean subtlety of tone
in a melodic mother lode of the tune's own
harmonic mine layered with a lover's pains

& even if must doubt those overseas troops
would've sent in '43 their constant requests
from Canal or carrier or bombardier groups
for K's rendition of that song Helen Forrest

sang with HJ's band soldier or sailor to ded-
icate its Hit Parade lyrics to the pretty nurse
or the sweetheart hoped still waiting to wed
her snapshot publicity would never disperse

as it had the Betty Grable iconic pin-up shot
of her leering back in her bathing suit so hot
with her Lloyd's insured million-dollar legs
Harry married that year of nostalgia & pegs

while Ken's therapeutic lines would as well
have rehabilitated limbs or a wounded heart
if his light staccato soothing at a lower level
it lingers longer to lessen loss & being apart

& if not Warren-Gordon's tune K's Willard
Robison "Old Folks" version they'd ask for
again after he & Roach had played it before
in the plaintive slow swing impossibly hard

for those never achieving his effortless ease
a crackling concise unflashy & ever sincere
cantando telling of a corn cob tale to please
& relieve to presto hope rallentandoing fear

if in his *Beggar's Opera* Gay seizes the day
sings "Beauty's a flower despised in decay"
his lyric itself as KD's album has yet to fade
as true songs survive on or off of Hit Parade

if in '55 "Mack the Knife" Satch's final side
on that disc first to reach high as number 20
sold a million plus & not until "Hello Dolly"
would hit top ten prior to the inevitable slide

Ken's of course cannot confuse with Louie's
whose vocal did the trick more than his horn
with its unmistakable its irrepressible breeze
ever blows its freshness & balm so unforlorn

letting forget for a moment a Brechtian shark
lying in wait with its pearly out-of-sight teeth
while K in modulating could dive underneath
to uncover light rays piercing a heartless dark

for as with Satch & Sonny Kenny too finding
even in such unlikely singing the silver lining
with Rollins in '56 turning a Weill's "Moritat"
from a deadly deed into his own colossal blat

K beaten to punch by the SR whimsical tenor
on that jaunty violent song as on the Debussy
& would be again in '57 by a Johnny Mercer
classic meant for Ken who outside the movie

of '36 when Bing had sung its satirical lyrics
knew *Rhythm of the Range* from real stirrups
no stunt-man routine of swingin' on a mount
& dashin' in a cloud of dust right out of town

& unlike Teagarden's "I'm an Old Cowhand"
of that same year with lipped trombone turns
& melodious cords punching the witty words
KD's a sophisticated give-&-take self-call-&-

response lyrical asking-answering dialogue
with bent flutter-tongued half-valved notes
conversing both with an Andy Adams' *Log*
& Westminster chimes to Parliament votes

taking serious the Big Ben ring where Jack
in his vocal played up JM's amusing rimes
ranged up-to-date in Ford V-8 not no hack
no doggies roped got along to beef betimes

not ever back home while Newk on his sax
trail driving with cutting honk rawhide lash
a swing man skirts the herd to have it think
it's unrestrained fully free to graze or drink

on January 10th of '60 K takes over the lead
rides the point in heading the steers to cross
on solid rock not into muddy creek at a loss
of weaker stock & to turn cattle's stampede

into milling ends the run then bedding them
down on Mercer's English tune a KD brand
seared on top converted to a hard-bop hymn
an anthem to remuda quirt & the Rio Grand'

& afterward had he recorded no other cover
still as such Goodnight Loving & Chisholm
hoofprints're bound to be followed by lover
of longhorn lore this track on *Arrival* album

ever to stand a landmark of KD's musician-
ship since it alone if no other will surely en-
dure for showing clear as wagon-wheel ruts
his inspired breath-release his blood & guts

yet album offers too K's own "Stage West"
chased at breakneck speed as if by outlaws'
gang or redskin raid & "Song of Delilah"'s
quieter muted Ken its "When Sunny Gets

Blue" showcase for Charlie Davis' baritone
leader's generosity become a second nature
though wish would've done it himself alone
except for rhythm as he did with the Mercer

& does with "Lazy Afternoon" as Flanagan
opens & closes with a hazy piano just quiet
enough to hear grass growing & daisies riot
melody lovelier muted unembellished plain

"Stella by Starlight" too on KD's quiet side
then with Manny Albam's funky "Six Bits"
K & Charlie totally together everything fits
another winner from a gambler true & tried

the same two horns hooking up in February
on 11th & 12th to record *Jazz Contemporary*
six tunes in stereo for Time "For those who
dare" plus "Sign Off" unreleased in "exclu-

sive sound extra" the label declares pianist
now Steve Kuhn & on its first three out of
six issued tunes Jimmy Garrison as bassist
but on "Horn Salute" "Tonica" "This Love

of Mine" it's again Butch Warren & drummer Buddy Enlow too as the month before Kuhn's piano K had heard as an instructor at the Lenox August '59 for Steve an alum

who then with Ron Brown comped behind Ornette & Cherry on "The Sphinx" & "Inn Tune" of Margo Guryan & then heard Ken tell all his students to be inquisitive to find

& learn every chord's formation in order to run its scale to break it up into what makes sense to get a rhythmic feel like land sakes alive so top to bottom all you'll play is you

true of K who practiced scripture preached as on his tune "A Waltz" on which he madly swings out of ¾ into 4 as alkali leached from ash for b'iled soap as the granger had

Ken's "breathtaking swoop" Mark Reilly's phrase "ringing" with "clarity & rich emotion" while Kuhn surprises with his tempo & feeling abruptly changed so fully please

if Charlie on bary squeaks a bit he was not K's first but his second choice since Heath couldn't make the gig but if Davis beneath leader's excitement level he isn't God wot

with a gruffish yet tender tone on his wondrous rendering of the Thelonious "Mood" "Monk's" i.e. a most moving solo for contemplation Kuhn's touchingly pensive too

the whole group tight & showing a proper
respect to one & all but K's show-stopper
chorus an authentic individuality "simmer-
ing" Reilly's word with Monkish signature

in handkerchief corner "designedly dropt"
as Walt brought to a boil by that Emerson-
ian thought & to compose his *Leaves* from
reading "The Poet" when universe stopped

but on "In Your Own Sweet Way" Charlie
can't get started with Brubeck's tune cov-
ered in '56 by Miles & 'Trane though KD
had not heard that earlier version with lov-

ing muted tones from Miles' harmon push-
ing Eros' button the tenor's sweeping licks
unlocking melodic line without romantic's
mush yet amorous in his caressive whoosh

K more playful but sticking close to theme
as Miles did to K too the melody the thing
by keeping away from clichés Bru staying
fresh & K said liked bary as other extreme

to his own high notes while Kuhn to prove
adventurous here & on KD's "Horn Salute"
with its "choppy jagged" military phraseol-
ogy Kenny knew yet better bop's "Crazeol-

ogy" Benny Harris's tune Bird had maybe
played for Pannonica in those hotel rooms
where K rehearsed & from there could see
the Hudson Jersey hills & whiff perfumes

used in her mixed-media paintings of milk
acrylic & Scotch did sketches then as Ken
& the men went over his "Tonica" written
for her as jazz Baroness whose Jewish gilt

took Monk in & who phoned a physician
then felt Bird's flickering beat heard thun-
der clap as doctor came too late musician
gone yet alive on walls sound never done

though neither K ensemble nor solo lines
seem to recall his former bebopping boss
whose choruses had gotten by heart signs
missing it meant to revisit her day of loss

on that weekend when she'd looked after
a ragged Bird watched TV when laughter
at juggler's act on Tommy Dorsey's show
broke blood loose choked & laid him low

March 5 '55 at Birdland in Ross Russell's
report Bud Powell's stewed Bird as well's
deep in his cups as Ken Blakey & Mingus
try to save the All-Stars date till KD tucks

his horn underneath an arm off to the side
of the cursing legends had befriended him
but now Ken cannot do the same for them
ill past his cure must just move on if cried

back then or here in this nearly 3-minute
gift to her only with Butch's wistful bass
but a throb no sorrowing sob nor a hint it
miffed him Bird had given Red his place

which leaves his CD's final piece his *sui*
generis rendition of "This Love of Mine"
with its fetching distinguished just lovely
tone his charming staccato so utterly fine

& same be said for the Harold Land date
of July 5th & 8th when as a stocking mate
perfectly matched to Houston-born tenor
San Diego-raised he & K one fitting pair

"so close" on their "So in Love" as Cole
Porter's lyrics say while Clarence Jones
on bass pushes & pulses & Ken's whole
solo's full of euphonious priceless tones

as he hits every note right on the money
undergirded on piano by an Amos Trice
a Joe Peters on drums two who not only
lend ample swing but more than suffice

with the pianist's own waltz the second
tune a piece he entitled "Triple Trouble"
& on which the horns together a fecund
duo sways in tune rich grain not stubble

on David Raksin's "Slowly" the tenorist
bringing out the theme of poignant love
then speeding it up for a blowing above
& beyond his solid work maybe his best

with Kenny more touching still yet light
in spirit as Trice turns in a splendid solo
of Clarence's bass chorus a simple ditto
then horns closing so romantically right

though "On a Little Street in Singapore"
it lacks aroma of a "lotus-covered door"
held in embrace by pale perfumed hand
no temple bells in K no exotica in Land

but back to their habitat in "Okay Blues"
can hear them at home with K's pinched
tone emotes in honor of Orrin Keepnews
here not a player would ever be benched

so KD arrived & on December 9th at last
tenor's Jimmy Heath piano Kenny Drew
bass Garrison drummer Art Taylor to do
another set for Time a Kern whistle blast

of light-hearted *Show Boat* tunes with all
aboard steaming along to Jerry's musical
play Hammerstein lyrics based on Ferber
novel of '26 his sidemen Ken would aver

the best he ever picked for any album yet
all hanging loose but with a surging drive
powers refreshened vibes bring love alive
in songs Jerome had to pen with no regret

can hear in any why K had wanted Heath
but most of all in "Bill" when the tenorist
nearly stealing the show soars flips twists
& turns till Ken returns to win the wreath

with shifting tacks as in trimming of sails
for running the bow into wind for sudden
directional change a self-conversing nails
close-hauled notes high to low his caden-

za a trophy-cup end to the tune & session
began with "Why Do I Love You" telling
piano comping percussion unpell-melling
& bass pulsing a steady tasty punctuation

as "full-throated" tenor a K "more supple"
to quote Nat Hentoff's insert notes groove
alone or together a complementary couple
wedded by & unto jazz may none reprove

on "Nobody Else But Me" KD's bending
of tones Jimmy'll answer with a blending
of matching bends each filled with a feel-
ing for love's root chords harmonies heal

on "Can't Help Lovin' That Man" a ca-
pacity for gentleness flows this an alter-
ing of Hentoff phrase with K's unfalter-
ing expressive force a lyric emotive ca-

ressive rush a Mississippi pouring forth
as Williams wrote on Hernando's corse
later Crane's "hosannahs silently below"
in nearing docks the paddlewheels slow

to "Make Believe" & a stevedore Drew
not stomping as Duke but over keys un-
loading a *Cotton Blossom* not forgotten
"dartingly humorous" ever fresh & new

K flawlessly states its still lovely theme
his nuanced shapes & shades surprising
so & as only its metal & reed can swing
Heath's tenor renews any lover's dream

then horns together on "Ol' Man River"
toting barge & lifting bale to lend relief
to past injustice but notes would deliver
for here & now their firmly-held belief

no self should wish to be someone else
& in riding the deepest current of Kern
to render in tones ideal & real & return
to dock revealing both within all selves

as Razaf in his "Christopher Columbus"
sighted by the sextant in a sailor's song
so KD came to see had not gone wrong
taking tune & lyrics as a truer compass

would bring him invitations from afar
to make a voyage with his musical tale
travel packed with a minor-blues scale
in head & fingers chord as guiding star

ran arpeggio calisthenics to keep in shape
two octaves at a time or blew whole tones
for toning of lips & lungs but in his bones
needed calcium of home to break the tape

must if but in spirit touch his native place
to retain its strengthening within his heart
& head strong so long as like old Antaeus
mythical son ever in contact never to part

from Mother Earth not until lifted into air
by Hercules then could strangle him there
choke that giant whose stomping grounds
renewed his sinews with KD's his sounds

on January 15 '61 doing BN *Whistle Stop*
seven pieces all Ken's own from "'Philly'
Twist" his wordplay upon an equine filly
& Joe Jones' sobriquet to Southwest pop-

art scenes of earthy "Buffalo" a "Sunset"
"heralds evening chill after a hot dry day"
"Windmill" water for splashing off sweat
a healthier brew than the beer or whiskey

with train of the album title harking back
to stops only made on station master flag-
ging it down for passenger without a bag
had packed clothes & grub in a flour sack

the other two tracks a "Sunrise in Mexico"
when Ken saw it the liner notes fail to say
though must've seen it for Ira's quoted K
on skies there so different seemed so low

& the session-ending "Dorham's Epitaph"
a short & poignant to-the-point 69 second
leave-taking eleven years prior to the fact
of his further music lost to a great beyond

with here again his cohorts Hank on tenor
& Kenny Drew piano while drums & bass
from Miles's '50s band had been together
& kept its driving time few if any outpace

that is to say Philly Joe's cymbals & skins
Paul Chambers' walking strings a winning
team to back up that pair of Kenny friends
from earlier dates a quintet all set to swing

his hemiola railway theme in the tradition
of Henry "Ragtime Texas" Thomas's pan-
piped blues his strummed guitar's itinerary
on the Katy line served his own Big Sandy

he names in song along with Grand Saline
& Silver Lake Marshall where K had seen
its freight cars rumble by & felt 'em shake
as a roaring Charlie Green trombone break

on '32 "Hobo You Can't Ride This Train"
with Louie a tough laughin' brakeman lets
after all the poor boy on begins with clang-
ing bell & within its limit of just 3 minutes

chugs with a timeless beat till Chick's wire
brushes slow the wheels now switch to '26
when Duke's "Choo Choo" stoked by Irvis
Greer & Miley's muted flutter-tongued fire

then '33 & Ellington's "Daybreak Express"
his lesser "Happy-Go-Lucky Local" of '46
followed one of his orchestra's biggest hits
the Strayhorn "'A' Train" an instant success

but did KD think of any of these or remem-
ber more a ticket Gil Fuller bought for him
on a coach down into Louisiana from NYC
in '46 to join the Eckstine band with Blakey

crossing at St. Louis that Mason-Dixon line
meant his seat changed from middle to rear
to the last car with only the caboose behind
next to a lunch pail a box perforated for air

in alligator on suede & his bebop horn-rims
K ready for a Southern tour on Mr. B's gigs
when farmers piled on with dead opossums
live chickens in burlap sacks squealing pigs

& later by bus broke down in snow in West
Virginia then on north to Pittsburgh in time
for Christmas dinner at Art & Billy's home
soon back with wife & first daughter at last

up from Dixie as those by underground rail
did K think he'd retraced that freedom trail
or in '61 recall more Monk's "Locomotive"
of '54 with Copeland on trumpet inventive

as ever & must've impressed Ken as much
as the piece's "train blues" rhythmic figure
Blakey's artful drums Frank Foster's tenor
& Thelonious' iterative sure-handed touch

certainly K's album has unity contrast too
with its sunrise bright & a mute to subdue
his syncopated slower setting yet reviewer
John S. Wilson got it right Derek's demur

did not since former judges K's ensemble
writing's provocative promise goes unful-
filled by tenor & trumpet solos offer only
stale warmed-over licks little new tonally

so even heroes may disappoint though K
charts still hold up as before his final say
he & Mobe bring back the bearded bison
wind in harness iron-horse & a rising sun

& would again on a June 14th to 15th date
tenor Clifford Jordan's *Starting Time* reis-
sued in 2001 but title then *Mosaic* pianist
Cedar Walton's tune he too of KD's state

Big D native as cited before in bebop line
though warmer toned a comper with taste-
ful unexpected fills & here especially fine
on K's "Sunrise" a rendition faster-paced

& far more satisfying as Clifford works in
to great effect Ken's Indian theme yet can
regret no solo by him can now admit even
miss the one taken in January 15's version

but find prefer his & Clifford's interaction
as in both beginning & ending it adds vari-
ety answers a critique of sameness Wilson
lodged also Cedar's parallel octaves apply

a Latin flavor with a classical flair as bass-
ist extraordinaire Wilbur Ware carries K's
piece with his rich acoustic drive & Albert
"Tootie" Heath's tom-toming motif expert

Ken's "Windmill" as well at a quicker clip
& in Gitler's notes it's rotating at a rate of
speed too great for the quixotic knight suf-
fered from gigantic sails in Sorcerer's grip

but a real wind spins K's Southwest pump
to water the herd on an actual Texas ranch
Clifford twirling to Wilbur's steady thump
lends to prairie life at least an even chance

& in his solo opens the side a fiery KD siz-
zles & burns is just as hot in his whirlwind
lines while tenor fanning no conflagration
rather taps a deep drink cools & quenches

though those came later & is skipping over
two '61 albums with Ken had come before
one led on March 13 by tenor Rocky Boyd
whose career after '62 has remained a void

as has after '66 the life of trumpeter Wilbur
Hardin who recorded with 'Trane in '58 on
his *Standard* date & then with Curtis Fuller
on a '60 session until fallen ill Lee Morgan

took his place & he in turn shot dead in '72
by his older longtime jealous female friend
Hardin possibly absent the scene from men-
tal illness dropped out as did trumpeter Du-

pree Bolton though he strung out on heroin
& from serving times worst in San Quentin
came after *The Fox* in '59 & *Katanga!* of '63
one with Harold Land & other Curtis Amy

on both a trumpeter blazing with technique
to spare only to die alone unknown no horn
listed among personal effects just a diabetic
with a 19-inch color TV not a soul to mourn

though Richard Williams a Brit would belat-
edly in '99 track Dupree down to Oakland's
county records couldn't forget his & Land's
"intellectual bite" his exceptional Amy date

needed to investigate & learn what it meant
to have heard an improvising musician play
one's bones blood & brain as an instrument
runs chills up spine stirs neurons sad or gay

why gifted prey to a darker side can deepen
attraction a listener feels for the fewer notes
has left behind guilt felt over pleasure given
by doomed to little pay gold arms or throats

Lee had kicked the habit helped by his killer
Wilbur an introvert departed without a trace
except for his warm tone on "Spring Is Here"
& on *West 42nd Street* his title tune with K's

chorus on the eighth take filled with his wry
concisely executed quip-like twisting & turn-
ing on "Ease It!" Rocky's solo showing why
on taking Mobe's chair with Miles he'd earn

comparisons with 'Trane & Rollins although
his three-month stint in '61 & this session of
that same year the only evidence & must suf-
fice as proof new star did rise before he'd go

with his own "Avars" starts things off nicely
enough & if modest his solo setting up a KD
now drives & swings at his best & on "Stella
by Starlight" the two each in his way to tell a

moving tale in loving sound & then on drum-
mer Pete La Roca's bow to Miles' "So What"
the unison horns rock out his own "Why Not"
to Ron Carter's walking bass fades to solemn

its last notes leaving in air an eerie modal feel
before the blues by Chambers where Ken will
"Ease It!" first in the lower gear then shifts in-
to high octane but comes to little Rocky's ten-

or engages more & may even be the case with
Luiz Bonfá's "Samba de Orfeu" Kenny heard
while in Brazil *that* Alun Morgan has averred
in his album notes though the date of that trip

came months later in July '61 when Ken went
to Rio with a group Dave Bailey led including
Al Cohn Zoot Sims Curtis Fuller & the fluting
of Herbie Mann part of a tour of the continent

Brazil Argentina Paraguay a fourth stop can't
say where with just the one CD from Rio per-
formance at Teatro Municipal & K's enchant-
ing version of "Autumn Leaves" a KD feature

piece with bass Bennie Tucker Dave's percus-
sion Ronnie Ball piano backing up K's stacca-
toed bent & half-valved notes in festive tocca-
ta style yet dolor-tinged as falls off deciduous

& on "Wee Dot" fluent K's flourishes flashes
& rapid-fire runs match Curtis's string of non-
stop motific tongued riffled trombone plashes
Al & Zoot's splashings to Ray Mantilla's con-

ga drum a ten-minute session of improvisation
on J.J.'s theme the time length too of "A Night
in Tunisia" where each vibration or detonation
from KD's horn its sound alone none can sight

yet lights up aural skies as if the Halley-comet
in title of Al Cohn's tune & even if K not on it
just on J.J.'s Dizzy's & Kosma's his a trumpet
in any unit on any song called could always fit

& from each discovered land would import its
sonic soul into & through his Texian horn hits
like his "Una más" "Blue Bossa" & Luiz Bonfá's
"Manhã de Carnaval" his famed *Black Orpheus*

theme from the '59 film K could have known
& too its Bonfá "Samba" even before the tour
the latter would record in '63 when had flown
to Copenhagen & after another gig with Fuller

Tucker & Bailey the KD October '61 *Osmosis*
included too Tommy Flanagan piano & as his
tenor man Frank Haynes a session Black Lion
cut in NYC with its title tune by Osie Johnson

also on Kenny's debut album of December '53
with Walter Bishop & Heath bros Jim & Percy
K quoting then in his too brief solo a Grieg mo-
tif but not repeating it here wasn't for doing so

ever trying something new at least now stretch-
ing out on a chorus if longer more ostentatious
& yet for all its higher lower notes not so fresh
as on that earlier intenser outing less ambitious

will an artist just naturally slowly grow mature
or suddenly change & become more adventure-
some for sure K choruses show greater control
but not always in service of thought as a whole

though more often better than had been before
if unlike now with a Haynes no equal to Heath
yet still a worthy cohort can manage to breathe
much life in his lines alluding to a tune in *Por-*

gy & Bess its "Summertime" o so sempiternal
& quotes too "It's Alright with Me" the Cole
Porter song with its image of a charming face
as in "Memory" by Yeats cannot take *her* place

& then Curtis the trombonist will pick up on it
as piano bass & drums all kick the horns along
Tommy's featured on "Just Friends" a favorite
of pianists Mark Gardner writes & isn't wrong

K stronger on "Soul Support" & "Grand Street"
in former saying something in a feeling groove
& the tenor too in the same soul vein no "Moving Out" of Rollins but as lyrics say "it's alreet"

"An Oscar For Oscar" KD had also done in '53
when if yet was immature & fertile ideas fewer
the fervid improvisation on his tune was newer
so palpable even if it lacked his later mastery

& of course in the company of thunderous Art
Parkerish Lou funky Horace compatriot Gene
K seems more at home & truly young at heart
& to be in November '61 with Jackie McLean

Leroy Vinnegar & Walter Bishop "once again"
Art Taylor too or as in that Spanish phrase Ken
uses as his lead-off tune for the *Inta Somethin'*
album its one more time "Una más" translation

a piece allows "for unusual flexibility of mood"
in his '63 words "from bossa nova to the blues"
as he & Jackie over syncopating piano do their
rhythmic solo thing once theme stated as a pair

each building to his own intensity of tonal wail
each squeezing & fluttering for a deeper swing
& on "It Could Happen to You" Ken fluttering
again then bends drops & drives the liquid nail

of a fluidity few could match though on ivories
Bishop approaches as fingertips ripple the keys
& then after "Let's Face the Music and Dance"
features Jackie's dashing sax K gets his chance

to show a warmly muted side on Loesser's "No
Two People" & then again after JM's alone for
"Lover Man" the forces join on "San Francisco
Beat" K's piece perhaps to the post-war author

horns & drum together hammer a declamatory
line as did those bearded poets would not con-
form take a bath shave go to work accept mon-
ey as any measure of life on their road to glory

yet Ken himself a clean-cut & dependable guy
raising with Rubina the five bright girls in-be-
tween his after-hours jobs record gigs for buy-
ing them seasonal togs each her birthday party

but in earning his living in a music field his sis-
ter's preacher spouse looked down upon did K
believe in its higher good as buddhist beatniks
did who heard in his jazz the enlightened Way

did K then think he had spent his days the best
he could or feel at times they had been a waste
unlikely he'd ever have lived with such regrets
but if so outweighed by mates on session dates

places his playing had taken him to distant dif-
ferent lands where foreign fans with eager ears
took the Texian in where color never interferes
nor impairs hearings of his rich heritage of riff

on April 15 '62 back in NYC after the Golden
Gate scene cable car rides Birdman's Alcatraz
later red-masked parrots of Bittner & The Jazz
Workshop where the quintet recorded live Ken

& Jackie on again but in United Artists' studio
with J.C. Moses drums Bobby Timmons piano
& Teddy Smith on bass for the album *Matador*
KD's title tune inspired by South America tour

after Brazil to Buenos Aires from there a motor
trip to Rosario on the river Paraná better known
in Argentina than either bullfighting or toreador
as are the Rosas dictatorship & a Borges *ficción*

where Ken may have heard & witnessed that rit-
ual death with its balletic moves banderillas fan-
fare's signal to kill the animal if its disconsolate
horn gore not before *el torero*'s sword blade can

remains unclear or whether KD might have read
García Lorca's "the sad breeze through the olive
trees" on an afternoon "all the clocks struck five"
when the poet could not stand to see blood shed

but if he neither knew the poem in native words
nor rendered into English verses never the same
K comprehended the "men who break [or tame]
horses & rivers" & spooked hoof beats of herds

& something of an elegant dancer gone & a cry-
ing crowd broke windows of their Sevillian sky
heard in his simple & repeated chords as before
him on modals a Miles Monk & 'Trane did soar

& he too & Jackie do with nuances will still sur-
prise while piano alludes to Diz's Tunisian night
as if to Arabic roots of centuries of stylized fight
in a Roman ring roaring *olé* at passes ever closer

then Jackie's three-part "Melanie" beginning al-
most as a classical piece with piano's deep bass
a pounding of eerie sinister vamps the horns fol-
lowing with a thematic wail on alto J's wordless

keen till Bobby J.C. & Teddy all to set a rhythm
swings & Kenny starts with staccato tip-toe run-
ning his fleet patented tonguing so under control
high to low a Bud Powell quote a coda with soul

a McLean chorus complements K's recalls open-
ing sepulchral tones & converts his reed to a ten-
or's lower vibe then of a sudden leaps to flurries
will relieve listener from minor & major worries

then more so on Chaplin's "Smile" where Ken's
at his falling-off fuzzy-toned happy best even as
an accelerating juggernaut of *Modern Times* has
caught Little Tramp in cogs of a Depression lens

since in silent film & in "There Goes My Heart"
comedian & singer go right on saved by a song
KD plays with inimitable timing & his own sort
of achy-breaky romantic charm lifts up & along

leaving for last a Villa-Lobos work his "Prelude"
Ken had heard Segovia the great guitarist strum
on a recording at Max & Abbey's place & from
then on planned to play it as a type of sad etude

& with just piano as Jelly Roll & King Oliver's
'24 duet on "Tom Cat Blues" or the Pops-Fatha
"Weather Bird" in '28 but KD with no improvi-
sation just lipping of exercise notes his answers

to Bobby's harp-like keyboard calls a wavering
as if of ripples on a lake then diving down & up
till ending on a held final higher peal a favoring
wind brings his trip full circle *fútbol* goal & cup

though in '62 Jackie & K would sail once more
on a June 14th Blue Note session later collected
on *Vertigo* with one of '63 when J had selected
Donald Byrd as KD's sub after that year before

when by then Ken's friend Joe Henderson & he
had begun a fruitful collaboration on Blue Note
too & he'd travel alone for playing in company
of Danes Swedes & Norwegians got KD's vote

but still in '62 would join with Jackie's rhythm
section of Sonny Clark as pianist Butch Warren
bass & Billy Higgins whose tuned drumming in
'59 swung Ornette's *The Shape of Jazz to Come*

& here too K would end where he started from
constructing solos return to themes as on drum-
mer's "Marilyn's Dilemma" Butch's "The Way
I Feel" to sum tie up & unify all he's had to say

K so accurate in stating tunes as on "The Three
Minors" Jackie's piece where the alto's horizon
now stretches out & as Sidran writes has clearly
broadened toward New-Wave *One Step Beyond*

but perhaps the critic's wrong in claiming Ken's
a papa of "the splatter school of trumpet playing"
even the altoist on bassist's tune is into meleeing
more than Ken sews close with a neat coherence

& on "Minors" he deliberately works out simple
patterns to uncover each intriguing combination
of rhythm & sound & on "Blues in a Jiff" to trill
with valve shake drop off note & flutter tongue

if his own "Blues for Jackie" can't compete with
Sonny's "Jiff" or Jackie's "Iddy Bitty" Ken makes
much more of latter's theme than even the altoist
does in the rather boring repetitious solo he takes

his effort's better on KD's tune but then K's own
beginning too much like licks had already blown
till cadenza of sorts heats up the chorus will win
him roses & accolades ought to have been given

when still alive but wasn't as Jackie in conversa-
tion with Ben Sidran for *Talking Jazz* later to say
ever too late's a tragic fact but then at least his re-
cordings survive to keep him one's contemporary

as forever among his peers as on '62's *Invitation*
Bags' August to November sessions on Riverside
with tenor Heath bass Ron Carter piano Flanagan
drums Connie Kay & Virgil Jones a trumpeter rid-

ing shotgun on only two out of its seven pieces K
playing lead to drive the Milt Jackson sextet team
more so than will improvise but does with a seam-
lessness can identify by a straight-ahead unhesita-

tion in every swinging phrase as a stagecoach out-
races bandit bullets or arrows of whooping braves
mostly on Thelonious' "Ruby, My Dear" yet saves
some fire for "The Sealer" to return it at any shout

& on Bags' tune "Poom-A-Loom" to foil a would-
be holdup man & to outshoot with mute Virgil's o-
pen tones but of his short "None Shall Wander" so-
lo did he feel its part in his larger chart not so good

as he seriously sought in writing music desired be-
yond his trumpet skill a sounding of its deeper title
with its biblical ring & even against it would travel
in search of song & the audiences for setting it free

Flamboyaning & "Our Thing"

not just another year but his finest yet
& with a bang it begins at Flamboyan
Queens nightspot with fewer at the set
on Monday January 15 than MC Alan

Grant could wish but happy to have K
D Quintet with Joe Henderson's tenor
Ronnie Mathews piano the drummer J
C Moses had been with Kenny before

& Steve Davis bass on WRFM's after-
midnight live broadcast of a chemistry
right as rain & as taped would capture
for later listeners Ken's soulful legacy

enhanced on "Dorian" by the pianist's
chords beneath his modal waltz whose
haunting theme K delivers with blues-
like low till sunniness lifts fog & mist

when his trills loping staccatos falling
off at ends of notes & a cooling-toned
breeziness come along as on installing
summer window fan bought or loaned

did he think of slaves & Aesop's fable
of tortoise & hare or mixolydian scale
syrinx Delphic Ptolemaic dithyrambic
Anacreontic Sapphic Pindaric the epic

Homer Heraclitus Herodotus Hercules
Hermes Hera Hippocrene Hippocrates
Pythagoras Plato Aristotle & Socrates
Aeschylus Aristophanes or Sophocles

or did K with horn in bare hands seek
a reply as W.C. Williams did to Greek
& Latin not, not certainly Ezra's clas-
sical paraphrase just Attic-styled jazz

the tenor then enters restrained at first
but slowly he builds to ecstatic shakes
his nearly unpleasant & painful bursts
yet to the point as apt music he makes

but not so consoling as Ken had made
or "squeezed" as Blumenthal phrased
his "full measure of emotion from" his
"every note" each "frayed at the edges"

& at the time his life too it seems from
loss of his cabaret card needed for jobs
kept out of venues in NYC by the cops
checking IDs charging with possession

whether hooked on the stuff or in a car
& busted together with junkie friend as
Monk'd been can't say & yet does mar
even if then an all-too-common in jazz

had at least in '63 his Blue Note record
dates & the clubs abroad would accord
him respect a greater crowd again than
here at home a hopeful alternative plan

at least Ken still being heard in Queens
& on the airwaves thanks to Grant who
after Duke/Gershwin hit says K "beau-
tiful tonight" know just *what* he means

for with tune Bunny swung bop Dizzy
too on "I Can't Get Started With You"
K adds his warm hard-bop bravura to
styles sang blew tribute to its melody

lilted by Billie who only changed lyr-
icist Ira's line so Basie took her to tea
not Gabriel after advising Franklin D.
Pres then in '37 & the same for Lester

like K Joe evokes the Gershwin words
his "garrulous tenor attack" a blowing
digs right in & Joe with Ken two birds
of a feather have this "vibration going"

& then on the brothers' "Summertime"
Kenny rarely better in his whole career
through his horn's entire diapason hear
a tonal range from blue to near sublime

& now the tenorist has come on strong
more assertive & thus the effective foil
with loquacious lines note choices long
on a farther exploration of theme a boil-

ing of honks & highs distinct from K's
more direct yet graceful flutter & half-
valved delicious intensity of tone stays
closer to song above or below the staff

& next comes the renamed "Una más"
its title's now "My Injun From Brazil"
version new & improved though April
1st recorded again with KD's compass

expanded from his statement of theme
if altered in accent not nearly so much
in form as a god changes into a stream
to get human girl in its Ovidian clutch

while now at club not Blue Note studio
Joe takes a long & a bit repetitious solo
at times strains for an effect till Ronnie
to the KD bossa beat swings every key

as K did on "Autumn Leaves" in Brazil
here he truncates his solo's time shares
it with his men a greater space or equal
to his own for knows a welcome wears

out overstayed self-abnegating minutes
never placed on him any creation limits
could say his say in fewer bars not a go-
ing on & on as others would & also Joe

for though tenorist could generate drive
his lines lack a K's coherence of work-
ing by way his overall thought to arrive
at each fitting note never going berserk

but then no sooner said than on K tune
"Dynamo" later titled "Straight Ahead"
his solo will run amok as tones oppugn
the all-inclusive assertion flatly refuted

by technique serves itself till piano en-
ters & comps to save the wayward Ken
from turning into his own worst enemy
for at times even best'll become or any

yet both men are generators & more so
on the later April Fools Blue Note date
as K's not kidding around on "Straight
Ahead" just JH quotes "The Merry-Go-

Round Broke Down" as Ken even cuts
his January nod to a Diz "Salt Peanuts"
for in getting down to serious business
convinces with lines like sales pitches

of kind Charles Ives would never give
too shy himself so written down for in-
surance agent in selling policy to deliv-
er instead this in between composition

of ragtime pieces *Two Contemplations*
or *In the Cage* a music more dissonant
than K might write yet each's enchant-
ing in a native way despite separations

by time & race both hearing America's
African rhythms as K includes samba's
"magic pulse" in "Una más" its slower
April version turning it even mellower

both composers provided for those sur-
vive & others to come with credit lines
assure well-being in any futures secure
from notes each had written for assigns

in a later age to read from page or play
through vinyl or compact discs like this
where Ken on his "São Paulo" stretches
out Joe with no "multi-directional spray"

Hentoff says & as to "incisive lyricism"
Kenny's inspired by "hallucinated city"
in '22 hosted Modern Art Week schism
broke with old to dragoon a new poetry

Ken's other sidemen here young Herbie
Hancock on piano Tony Williams drums
along with Butch Warren his bass in '60
on K *Arrival* album but plucks & strums

better now with strings state "bittersweet
wistfulness" of KD's "home-grown 'bos-
sa nova'" theme the real thing no "effete
cocktail lounge" treacle (Cuscunan gloss)

then shouts Count Basie "one more time"
which recalls Futurist works of Bandeira
Andrade & Meireles' piano-tuner rhyme
nota/remota "Little Train of the Caipira"

of Heitor the romantic warmth the color
of vibrant Brazil aswirl in his memories
for weeks to come in a bit of Portuguese
then session ends with no ballad lovelier

Camelot's "If Ever I Would Leave You"
as his trumpet fall flutters to lower notes
his alone not like any from other throats
floating on Herbie fills even if KD knew

was not to receive recognition deserved
yet he & his sidemen closing with grace
& however it went Ken never unnerved
tells Nat he's satisfied anytime he plays

& will do so June 3rd for Joe's *Page One*
with "Recorda Me" a tune by Henderson
fits right in with K's famed opener "Blue
Bossa" though tenor's nova not then new

written in '55 predated K's the fact men-
tioned in album liner notes Kenny wrote
depict the tenorist as a musical astronaut
launched from pad by his rhythm section

a three-man crew of again Butch Warren
on bass but Pete La Roca their drummer
& McCoy Tyner piano each a newcomer
to Joe & K Quintet never quite the same

though the horn duo's known right away
by the trumpet's flutter & tenor's flurries
Ken by as Monk recommended his stay-
ing close to his theme who rarely hurries

just takes his time finding nuanced tones
while Joe at his best digs deeper & sticks
to a consistent groove with buoyant licks
in keeping with K's melody Tyner hones

then after Ken's bossa his ballad up next
entitled it "La Mesha" for their youngest
daughter just three years old but in 2008
at an Austin Music Memorial better-late-

than-never tribute to her father's sounds
his lovely lady as a child inspiring Joe's
three uninhibited choruses then K solos
in meditative mode not leaps or bounds

next taking off on "nothing but a blues"
own description of Joe's "Homestretch"
by pacing himself as the track star sets
a record time the tenor lapped on cruis-

ing by when K in no mad dash crosses
line & breaking its ribbon medals first
as La Roca paradiddles a *batería* burst
trades as if a baton bar to cut J's losses

but then Joe's "Recorda Me" can't live
up to K's translation as "remember me"
since words he heard on Rio street give
his blue bossa a better beat & harmony

just as here too Kenny in his solo works
his ideas out with attractive gliding glis-
sading tones like ballet of tongue & lips
an agility cannot forget no clumsy jerks

& on Joe's "Jinrikisha" he takes listener
on two-wheeled rickshaw of firecracker
dragon lady oriental ride black cat style
K popping alluring strings all the while

the session ends with "Out of the Night"
final Henderson tune but not worth writ-
ing home about even KD playing clams
no backhand winners & no grand slams

yet just "page one" of Joe & KD's book
to continue September 9th with a second
Blue Note date for the tenorist KD con-
sidered major league & even if J a rook-

ie then in '63 still to K he "indubitably"
among "most musical young saxophon-
ists to show since" a Yard had come on
& even if friends do speak in hyperbole

K did undoubtedly mean & did believe
the claim he made even if the record it-
self in telling a differing tale contradict
him & Feather's notes on its BN sleeve

Leonard's that is on tenorist's unpleas-
ing sound but no "ugliness for ugliness'
sake" just "big & forceful" yet unpleas-
ing even so & a sound ugly nonetheless

though still the critic's correct to praise
the way together they breathe & phrase
heard on their *Our Thing*'s "Escapade"
the album's final KD tune it too played

by the two as one & though at first here
again in his solo Joe below a KD's level
yet then slowly enters the piece's subtle
mood his best effort by far a singer peer

but still & all the exception since J more
often to lose his way fail to finish before
he leaps away in search of an impressive
high or low ever sidetracked ever restive

his own "Teeter Totter" the opening tune
with pianist Andrew Hill setting the tone
of seesawing up & down a dissonance on
top while running beneath a lyrical croon

La Rocan drums an upper tenor downer
even if his trill in Leonard's words "were
twisting a tiger's tail" then Ken's intense
yet notes empty just sound lacking sense

both horns far better on "Pedro's Time"
K's medium-paced tune a minor mellow
groove ever his best & his "wistful" solo
more representative with its dip & climb

than before on the tenor's opening track
with here now high-low intensity means
as he runs the gamut as if white & black
keys a needed contrast in various scenes

sonic statements the ears take in for real
while Joe is more focused meanders less
grabs the attention with phrases can feel
& Hill's "pretty obliquity" does impress

yet is it neither here nor there compared
to the horrors of war sufferings unheard
exploited poor ignored when only cared
to listen for note & chord is it all absurd

five grown kids just bumping their butts
on landing the playground seesaw board
deepening in sand their meaningless ruts
but still the thrill on being lifted upward

how not approve their creative urge over
& against destructive drive of such rover
as Indonesian the Somalian hijacks ships
taking of tanker crews & lives of tourists

for Joe's "Our Thing" title tune of album
carries to Feather no "overtones" of mob-
ster rule is a far cry from a high-seas rob-
bery a "gambit" rather gains momentum

by alternating to six-eight bars from four
the horns together stating the theme to o-
pen & close in perfect accord sadly more
inspired than either player's ho-hum solo

but both on track on Ken's "Back Road"
a down-home medium-gaited march-like
swinger with Joe slowing to an easy hike
then K in his exciting double-time mode

executing quick to the rears terrific direc-
tional shifts wide variety of tonal attacks
till cockeyed Hill will conduct an inspec-
tion for blues voicings in funky barracks

then a furlough from the troops & Joe
when in December '63 K's off for lands
of jazz fans in Scandinavian ice & snow
ardent Denmark Sweden Norway bands

all to welcome a man they count among
the music's upper echelon protégé if not
of equal rank of Bird or 'Trane yet allot-
ted his bebop portion & his praises sung

Traveling Again

first up is a Copenhagen Montmartre set
with Tete on keys Rolf a second trumpet
"the Great Dane himself" a just 17 Niels-
Hennig on bass & drumming Alex Riel's

all caught live on radio tapes from Miles'
"Solar" starts things off horns in tandem
the two as one till on his own Rolf's him-
self Ken none other unalike in solo styles

for when alone R's muffled tone to give
away it's he who takes his choruses first
right after its theme yet Sheridan asserts
it's K when an R grace note's distinctive

the sound not nearly so warm as K's nor
"emphatic" as even Chris observes a sun
effect not of stroke nor glare but's closer
to benignant rays in a photosynthetic run

later could've heated White House water
through panels installed at Carter's order
removed by Bonzo traffic controllers too
K's green energy might've aided jetBlue

with Dizzy's "Woody'n You" K maybe
tries too hard to prove could play "any-
thing" as liner note claims & if he most-
ly strains one burst carries off that boast

yet then when the horns chase with Alex
both as mousetrap lady protest too much
blow flurries cold as those outdoors rush
about like headless hens' bleeding necks

even Ken lost it now & again but picked
it up riding right on as Green Knight did
& here he does on "Scandia Skies" writ-
ten as mentioned before in honor of visit

lovely lines made lovelier still by his un-
derstated melodic plaint elicits spontane-
ous cry of the listener's unable to restrain
himself on hearing Ken's refraining from

ostentatious notes with the cracked inten-
sifying emotive force of his holding back
though swinging until Tete's complemen-
tary "ebullient restraint" & then the "stag-

gering" break by the teenage bass when K
returns to close as only he with his "essen-
tial wistfulness" ever could on endings en-
dure move once more in hearing him play

& equally with "It Could Happen to You"
where he'll keep coming back to discover
in its melody he's kept in mind a new nu-
ance enhanced with a trill staccato flutter

while Rolf adds his contrastive voice has
its say & if maybe a bit too cutesy "talks"
with great technique yet KD ever "stalks"
trumpeters showing off just chops in jazz

or depend on "bombast" as Sheridan says
in his note on *Short Story* Ken's title tune
"avoids" any "unnecessary" inflated ways
the word conveys just relied on by a goon

not KD nor Allan paired with him on flue-
gelhorn for the Danish radio December 19
airing from premier *jazzhus* & once again
backed up by the Pederson-Riel-Montoliu

rhythm section same as a fortnight before
the two horns together both on the money
note for note then thinking Ken to explore
with laidback legato strains not for punny

play on pop-song phrase but steps serious
as "displacement of melodic & rhythmic"
pace leads to sudden unheard-of terminus
by logic best belongs to thoughts in music

if immaterial feel when "tension released"
with ears taste all but a "bittersweet tang"
to "figures bunched" as if of grapes hang-
ing with arbor leaves an aural visual feast

then Botschinsky's tone a mellow autum-
nal harvest moon with ideas matching K's
& followed through to a fruitfulness from
warm & fluid lines this young Dane plays

far better than Rolf's & more in harmony
with Kenny's own & here too Tete offers
a chorus of richer thought fills the coffers
with a coinage or currency is never phony

but regret to say on "Bye Bye Blackbird"
K's wrongfooted he never gets untracked
taking the tune too fast to stampede herd
tramples Miles's '56 theme a painful fact

& even though after Alex solos K'll finish
strong it's way too late to make up ground
& will end up far back in a running Davis-
Coltrane led with their easy-driving sound

catches his breath on "Manhã de Carnaval"
to "air his elegant melodic powers" stating
the bossa with a tone so "poised" no rating
would do it justice nor a K funk so integral

an Allan feature's next "The Touch of Your
Lips" & wonder did K hear him a whipper-
snapper or admit his phrasing fine a humor
tasteful note choices right-on hardly a boor

or did Ken think then had passed his prime
as he sat listening to a new generation hold-
ing forth or still feel he had it in him no old
man at 39 but still could duel them anytime

& proving it then on "My Funny Valentine"
& if not wholly besting Botschinsky's flue-
gelhorn & its "round softly contoured" line
K never as Al lost in a maze without a clue

as that latter becomes after even laid down
a telling thread only to lose it before reach-
ing to where the labyrinth began a Theseus
with a killer tone yet no exit strategy found

though KD could always work his way out
of jams in choruses would get himself into
at least from one in "I Concentrate on You"
on Stockholm radio December '63 can tout

his coming back strong after a Lars Sjösten
piano solo for his final bars after had gotten
tangled in spots in an earlier chorus to show
with highest notes ever he can still really go

& before that with his sextet of former mate
Sahib Shihab on bary from '47 Blakey band
plus pianist Lars & Björn Alke another great
bass Bertil Lövgren trumpet & Bo Skoglund

drums to outswing Danes-Tete combo's ver-
sion of Ken's "Short Story" for the Swedes'
rhythm section's bursting its seams as feeds
the soloists with steam as does bigger fuller

ensemble sound of baritone & big-toned bass
& KD burns as almost never before or hardly
ever & if not up to him Bertil still in the race
never lets up goes after Ken with no timidity

tests himself against one of the best his range
& technique more impressive on their closing
piece Shihab's "Not Yet" where the imposing
power of Swede's attack isn't passing strange

no more than the announcer's perfect pronun-
ciation of titles in English Cole Porter's even
in between in Swedish introduces Sahib num-
ber when K's aggressive staccatos into some-

thing else his fresher in-the-face pressure propelled by an unrelenting Alke bass & Sahib so engaged much more now than on "Short Story" Björn bowing solid yet Lars no match for Tete

& Bo with his longest break a little repetitious but leads up to a final dramatic note screeched by a trumpet if not by KD's alone had reached this high mark aided by Shihab & the Swedish

although "not yet" so high as one awaited ears & eyes at that Golden Circle club where too in '63 Ken would & can be seen both by listeners seated there & at home on a computer's screen

not just his image pictured on record sleeves or next to liner notes on jacket backs or on a page in the booklet for a compact disc of on-line age decades after he'd gone shot by Bob Parent for

the '53 Debut vinyl with K wearing coat & tie from above his trumpet facing right his fingers on horn as blows or's only posed one in '55 by Francis Wolff for a 2-disc set with Messengers

in '56 for his *Prophets* cover by Alan Fontaine with instrument printed in yellow-gold his left side in profile & in black-&-white his checked sports shirt eyes closed & that same year again

caught in the act but then for Max's *Plus Four* once from the back standing with the drummer seated facing viewer once as K leans over in shot of him conferring with leader chum-

to-chum going over charts at the studio session
another of Kenny & Sonny blowing so intently
pictures all preserved to provide an impression
of living men through a Chuck Stewart artistry

photos by Paul Weller for '57's *Jazz Contrasts*
in one sitting on stool dressed in shirt & slacks
smiling with trumpet in hand serious in second
erect in a blue suit props right foot on top rung

Betty's harp beside him his gaze straight ahead
as in '58 shot for that same photographer's lens
focused on lady looks admiringly up into Ken's
big round eyes or at his porkpie hat & sharp red

tie for cover of his *This Is the Moment* & in '59
Esmond Edwards too had him stare from under
a similar brim for *Quiet Kenny* with its wonder-
ful ballads & blues would deeply & richly mine

Don Schlitten in '60 for album with "Cowhand"
took a frontal view reveals his right cheek slight-
ly puffed as he aims his horn at bottom of frame
though no sound issues through shadows & light

& for *Whistle Stop* of '61 Frank again to furnish
the cover photo of a pair of profile shots the one
with mouth more open & teeth in a smile versus
exact same pose but an all-but-closed expression

two sides of any man happy or sad his music too
yet each photographer only able to register silent
Ken imply his play its mood extrovert or reticent
while the Gyllene Cirkeln video can hear & view

whereas to see KD & Bird must listen to a record
from '49 & imagine their interacting & breathing
together or just from a still in '60 to fast-forward
to that Rebel stage can't hear K with the seething

Ornette won't ever know how he fit in with free-
jazz vanguardist from only a print as no tapes ex-
ist to replay its moment from fleeting time a Tex-
as intertwined tonal nexus lost forever to History

& so treasure the more a footage from Stockholm
& its cameraman panned that club where couples
with food & drink rapt or applauding sit at tables
as KD combines bebop skill & hard-bop emotion

dazzles with Doug Ramsey says on clip runs 1:25
"some of his most astonishingly beautiful playing"
& on cut of 2:19 from "Short Story" coming alive
as never before & to see him even with a relaying

of sound out of sync with image of fingers & face
can't ruin the effect of watching his muscles work
his puffing & perspiring as his lips on mouthpiece
relax tighten open let in breaths keep rhythm perk-

ing as tap-dancing fingertips on pearl-like tops of
valves run a scale or punch a short harmonic note
till returns to a theme it seemed he favored above
all others then & in year to come though anecdot-

al evidence can't confirm yet based on times he'd
record the tune in Scandinavia & once back home
then ends to audience applause the goateed Swede
announcing the piece just heard's alerted by wom-

an in tinted glasses seated with him K's beginning
to speak then see/hear him say the group will play
"Sky Blue" another tune of his starts off with ring-
ing cymbal seen as drummer taps it but gives way

to left hand of Leif Wennerstron strikes the snare
& then to Goran Peterson fingers strings on stand-
up bass behind a frontal view of K with one hand
holds up horn as other's middle digits press so air

be sent to tubes bring out such *sans pareil* sounds
when pianist Goran Lindberg taking his solo turn
nods his head to rhythmic lines he neither pounds
nor romps on a keyboard hear but cannot discern

from the camera angle as KD's shown waiting pa-
tiently snapping fingers keeping time to the piano
& bass's beat his horn held hanging down as solo-
ist swings then lifts his trumpet & prepares to play

the theme again after bassist will finish his chorus
& thus to end a unique priceless piece of cellulose
of KD in amazing acetate motion brings to a close
his major year of '63 yet not a sojourn so glorious

in decades before had appeared in film
in '48 or so it is said in *A Song Is Born*
but if KD is in a scene it must be when
Buck from dancer team picks up a horn

& acts the part of playing it in a jam on
"Flying Home" the '42 hit of Hampton
made Illinois & Arnett's tenors famous
for their Texas honks but here it's Louis

Tommy Dorsey Charlie Barnet & Hamp
himself with Danny Kaye on kettledrum
outwit the gangster sits holding a gun un-
derneath an oval *objet* falls as they ramp

up the swing till "sympathetic vibration"
rolls it off a shelf & hits him on the head
saves Virginia Mayo as a moll from wed-
ding the mobster boss its comic situation

saved by real jazz from Benny Satch Mel
Powell & on his vibraharp mostly Lionel
but if there at all K unheard with his tone
& technique's never weak so ever known

as is Dvorak *New World* "Going Home"
by vocal quartet & its mockingbird song
or Grieg "Anitra's Dance" Buck boogie-
woogies "at piano" as if to forecast a KD

in Norway after Sweden that film before
even his many quotes of Edvard's theme
in solos prior to his visiting Randi Hultin
in Gartnerveien & Oslo Metropole in '64

no cinematic club where Cavanaugh Trio
backs up Honey Swanson that role Mayo
plays as "dizzy dame" "only filly in stall"
sings of Basin St. blues by way of jungle

but Ken *is* in '59 *Les liaisons dangereuses*'
nightspot scene as decadent Paris elite
dance to Art Blakey's Messengers' beat
yet K is only shown with a horn he uses

as Vadim's movie prop since sound com-
ing out a pre-recorded Lee Morgan trum-
peted "guttural cry" on cynical plot near-
ing denouement revenges its love veneer

underscored by Monk theme Rouse & he
repeat each time Valmont & Juliette's de-
ceitful seducing plans take another shape
did K consent to fake it did a sort of rape

take place by need of bread did he expect
mistakenly to play music of Monk just as
in '59's *Un témoin dans la ville* he incorrect-
ly envisioned his future in playacting jazz

but for that Eduardo Molinaro thriller flick
did perform its sound-track score with four
cohorts Frenchman Barney Wilen on tenor
& soprano sax who also composed its slick

repeated motifs for chase in metro & S.O.S.
to radio-taxis but what's much more impres-
sive is his funky evocative theme uncharac-
teristically whose notes Ken at first'll crack

yet his tone & fluttering do add to Barney's
tune as do his wistful notes refer to movie's
tragic deaths & too a special KD tonal rich-
ness imparted to a *vie* motif in spite of slips

on music cut out of film Frenchman's saxes
lend to plot's love & murder their seductive
flow most of all on *melodie pour radio-taxis*
on *antenne* blues & *n'est qu'une lutte* to live

Duke Jordan on piano to cast a moving spell
just before Ken comes in at the end & closes
with scene at zoo Duke's solo none he poses
his improvising for real & really super swell

which seems to say K's film career went no-
where much one view of him can't compare
with that Swedish video nor even with pho-
tos from other years nor Randi's shot where

he's on a phone in her Norway home speak-
ing with whoever it is with lawyer tomes on
a shelf behind as he grins & shows his teeth
white straight & ever held his touching tone

at his visit did Randi's 12-year-old daughter
Wivi-Ann dance for Ken as she did for Bud
Dexter & Barney Bigard she had taught her-
self her mother avers jazz dance unheard of

in ballet shoes & tutu it's for sure K did sit
at the piano to play & sing a song was writ-
ten by Bud she had always thought till saw
a '59 copyright registered it to Ken by law

dated five years before K had sung for her
its notes & lyrics she taped in January '64
& in '85 film *Round Midnight* Chet Baker
to sing its words & music Gordon as actor

of Bud Powell's part but instead of piano
plays on tenor one more KD movie credit
his "Fairweather" of together ending hate
planting good-deed seeds for love to grow

if he watched Wivi-Ann must've brought
to mind his five girls awaited at home for
Ken's return but wouldn't be back before
recorded "Short Story" again was caught

by Jacques Bisceglia in sorta turban garb
enwrapped his head & worn against Nor-
wegian cold his throat covered by a scarf
bright eyes & smile for the photographer

warmed too by Norse Tore at piano bass
Björn & drummer Jon as named in chap-
ter one but no other tunes except in case
of J.J. Johnson's "Lament" if KD unhap-

py with poor quality of sound was surely
pleased with the way he & sidemen play
his own "Sky Blue" the solos all securely
taken by Ken & his rhythm section array

on Diz's "Con Alma" K sings with soul
only departs from its simple yet moving
theme for ingenious licks each soothing
hearing K's held notes leaves one whole

their superlative version of "Short Story"
shows again that his tune must've been
at this or at any time a favorite with Ken
here Tore's at his best & as for Björn he

too digs in & from beginning to end Jon
comes on stronger than ever as he wails
on drums helps to hammer home K son-
ic highs & lows drive his hard-bop nails

then after one unheard February session
with Dexter Gordon KD's back in NYC
& on March 21st to fit in after a fashion
with leader Andrew Hill & Eric Dolphy

for *Point of Departure* the most far-out
diaphonic date Kenny would ever make
as pianist's long angular solos all about
escape from anguish & solitude his tak-

ing "Refuge" in post-modern dissonant
tonal centers rather than keys & chords
if K's partly out of place in a vanguard's
abstract truth Andrew totally confident

he could do the job & does contribute
greatly to playing of Hill's demanding
themes & on "Spectrum" K with mute
& Eric flute set down a perfect landing

yet Dolphy on alto & bass clarinet flies
beyond the rest in his eccentric squeak-
ing swing brings in a fleshly feel defies
gravity the ascetic Andrew would seek

while KD's best on their alternate take
of a Monkish "New Monastery" where
even within Hill's austerity Ken'll fare
as well as any but rejected for the sake

of an angrier more aesthetic statement
in keeping with times & then on Hill's
"Dedication" the wah-wah section fills
K's eyes with tears for his piece meant

in Andy's words "to express great loss"
here Henderson soloing better the boss
on piano's quite moving in his vertical
mode & just as they KD's more lyrical

though Nat felt could be themselves in
their penultimate "Flight 19" or in any
other Andy tune & even if even Kenny
had said to him he'd liked their session

"so much because had made him think"
& made him to "play in new directions"
yet the avant-garde not really K's thing
since hard bop his with few exceptions

for one on Henderson's '64 *In 'N' Out*
of April 10th with K's "Brown's Town"
where after horns blend in solid sound
in KD's solo he seems so full of doubt

confused perhaps by that date with Hill
his wrong foot first & to rely too much
on tired funky phrases serve as a crutch
his "Short Story" even on a lower level

than when had done it with the Swedes
Norse & Danes its beginning & ending
not the same the opening rhythm feeds
into a different feel leaves Ken tending

to stumble about while Joe on tenor to
clown a bit with KD's theme & Tyner
on piano to treat its tune rather lighter
than Scandinavians did would ever do

but even so never one to rest on laurels
tried new approaches to his older tunes
& if hung up KD never turning quarrel-
some or frowning like wrinkled prunes

nor gave up whenever going got rough
as on Joe's "Punjab" where tenor's best
hews to the Asiatic theme not in a huff
but with urgency as Heckman suggests

while K to meander in its bluesy mood
to a final striking passage though finds
no cluster of caves no echoing "boum"
brings Adela imagined rape & reminds

too of *Jewel in the Crown* Muslim Sikh
independence partition two sects wreak-
ing havoc still never into their religious
hate just boppish Indian-Pakistani licks

on "Serenity" he solos first & touches
with final notes unsettle a bit contrary
to title JH chose as if Ken rather wary
the state exists not a romantic mushes

the tenor mostly straight ahead not am-
biguous as Ken while Tyner too works
out a certain melancholic strain a dram
slightly calms if it hauntingly unnerves

& as for "In 'N' Out" cannot believe sax
& brass blend so well double the éclats
when J & K negotiate the tricky theme
& repeat it to end a pyrotechnic dream

still that commercial date cannot com-
pare with a distortion-plagued tape re-
cording of K with Tootie Heath drum-
mer Julian Euell on bass pianist Barry

Harris at HARYOU concert August 21
a month after riot of "Burn baby burn"
when teen shot by off-duty policeman
led to fires set lootings the Act in turn

funding Harlem Youth Opportunities'
Project Uplift the LBJ Great Society's
antipoverty pre-school remedial drop-
out plan the Film & Sound Workshop

invited Ken & his men when he'd in-
troduce the crowd to "Confirmation"
Bird's tune played with him at Royal
Roost February 19 '49 his horn a foil

to the master's dazzling swirling alto
with Kenny starting his own solo off
with a "particularly pretty phrase" so
Loren has said & if not his own doff-

ing his hat to the composer he quotes
but in '64 after K says Bird an ending
of an era in music history a beginning
of a new he rushes it hurries his notes

unlike fifteen years before but then in
fours with Heath his phrases more un-
der control its speed not affecting him
as it isn't on Barry's right-handed run

then K announces next the 1921 tune
"Ma He's Making Eyes at Me" opens
with fine Harris intro & even if Ken's
trumpet sound's blurred to begin soon

he will make up for it with a staccato
rivals not ever to copy patented or no
& on "'Round Midnight" the real KD
would have made the Monk so happy

if he heard how masterfully & loving-
ly K states timeless TM theme & em-
bellishes it with his uniquely moving
tones articulated as if it were a hymn

while backing him up each Harris fill
adds telling talk as no other K pianist
ever did & makes it more lamentable
this version is on no major label's list

having now traced part of the heritage
had alluded to in his opening remarks
after Parker & Monk K turns the page
to the Davis tune says for New York's

bands their closing "Theme" & here K
into his laidback thing for doesn't rush
& with his timing the greatest in a pay-
ment of homage to that too jazz genius

& last but not least to Dizzy's "Tin Tin
Deo" he Chano & Fuller in a collective
heads together gave to such ears as live
to hear it here shouts of encore till Ken

obliges with his cool hard-bop whizzes
encapsulate hereditary lines from Diz's
prowess & processing speed to Miles's
introspective harmon-nuanced analysis

on September 4th while a special music
consultant to & an occasional rehearsal
conductor for the HARYOU-ACT big
band K to cut *The Fox* would be a final

time an album billed as his & even with
eight more years to go & in most the six
at least to come his power undiminished
growing still & in a personal renascence

Hentoff says in liner notes with K's an-
swer to the question of his recent growth
"if you keep on living you have to" both
grow & "keep your ears & feelings open"

& showing it now with his fanfare proc-
lamation on his Afro-Latin titled "Trom-
peta Toccata" with its moods vary from
assertive to a morose takes-it-back rock

& his virtuosic display of technical skill
with its latino feel had cultivated before
if not from corrida trumpet for toreador
for sure after he'd heard bossa in Brazil

next comes Joe with a focused solo ful-
fills Ken's early expectations of tenor's
promise but Richard Davis nearly bores
with bass chorus like cruelty to the bull

till thankfully K returns to end as began
with a somber comedown from highs to
flutter as bassist bows & slurs for a blu-
er tone with on piano Tommy Flanagan

& now it's K's "Night Watch" although
there's no real darkness here for KD not
the morbid brooding sort if ever felt low
didn't play its part nor bemoaned his lot

even if wistful as Nat has written Kenny
looked forward to dawn more often light-
hearted as here in his solo almost jaunty
yet bluesy too as Tom on black-&-white

keys Joe's "Mamacita" a piece of Silver
since tenor's in Horace's band just then
his funkiness a harking back to Messen-
gers days while K if a bit pensive never

depressed a thinking man could open up
imbibe the good or bad sad or joyful cup
drink it to its wholesome or its bitter lees
knew either not just the sweet can please

his title tune occurred to him courtesy of
Davis's foxy look recalled his Texas roots
when he & friends had trapped as youths
that henhouse varmint none caring it suf-

fered on being caught just wanted its hide
nailed to a board & stretched until it dried
his theme more like the chase in the Pearl
poet's tale from the age of knight & churl

as Joe & KD dart & dodge & double back
to hunting horns & hounds howl in a pack
wily fox-like windings to outwit & delight
while Gawain too tries to escape his plight

if fates of critter & Sir to differ in the end
Ken's would too but from a Nat prophecy
"as variable a future as he'll want it to be"
for even though he still has plenty of wind

in him & goes right on as a highly sought-
after sideman-trumpeteer it won't be sky's
the limit as he envisions when his thought
says "there's more I feel I can do" then buys

into that Hentoff view of the rosy all ahead
but would not come true as Kenny in years
were left to him to follow where others led
as a leader if underrated never by his peers

Summiting

if he ever held hard feelings left unsaid
on 3/27/65 took part in a Carnegie Hall
concert marking the ten-year memorial
of a gone Bird *he* not his music is dead

debts to its time-timbre are still unpaid
though K with others owed him played
dues in tribute to that main bebop man
blew minds of musicians & many a fan

among those knew CP in flesh & blood
were upstaged by him in a live club set-
ting or studio recording session his bud-
dy Dizzy from that original '45 Quintet

Tommy Potter from the period of Miles
prior to Ken then Roy Haynes from '49
with Bean Bird's precursor in tenor line
Diz's James Moody Konitz of Capitol's

Evans & Davis '48-'50 *Birth of the Cool*
Gil cracking the whip in each rehearsal
Lee unaccompanied on his own "Blues
for Bird" an alto bearing Tristano news

then joins Taylor Potter KD J.J. "Siegel"
& Diz for solos & a jam on the Hawk's
"Disorder at the Border" of '44 official-
ly for the reader into historical thoughts

cut at the 2nd of 1st bop sessions held 22
February with world war winding down
whose dying would till its end continue
as from the cartels' killings here & now

after Billy's left-hand counterpoint line
in the pianist's "Bird Watcher" homage
rouses the crowd & leads into the unag-
ing bass solo Tommy takes K to remind

how far he'd come since Bird had fired
him back in '51 when instead had hired
Red his fellow addict served time in jail
but none of it's heard in K's happy wail

rooted still in a Bird's chimerical flights
yet as Hentoff says K's "humming-bird
facility of before" the Texan now unites
with his "fresh inventiveness" preferred

to running changes with a same old ring
lends no hint for dealing with inevitable
downward turn of fortune's fickle wheel
& unlike Diz K's eschewed bop quoting

whereas Gillespie tosses off a bugle call
Ken may have felt by then a bit cornball
for perhaps found in Diz's solo the high-
noting a gratuitous show no reason why

yet even so Dizzy still blows up a storm
& at the end with two trumpets together
pair blending distinctive sounds to form
as K with any horns fine windy weather

on 5/5/65 joins Jimmy Heath Ensemble
performing at Baltimore's Morgan Col-
lege where leader introduces on terrible
mike & after he says so K's feature fol-

lows with his version of "Be My Love"
slurred at first as if inebriated then later
clears as feels his way into his brand of
lyrical yearning then a swinging greater

by its relaxed yet intensely loping lines
than four-to-five minute solos taken by
Pepper Adams on bary & altoist Sonny
Red on their unannounced piece opens

in medias res with both coming on too
strong to force their repetitious figures
while after baritone's break KD ushers
in refreshing licks not a few quite new

& his solo shorter by ninety seconds or
even more & after Red choruses Cedar
Walton builds up to his fine conclusion
with bassist Reggie Workman & drum-

mer Roy Brooks driving the pianist on
Heath's unheard till after KD's feature
part of medley continued by J on tenor
leaves a touching technical impression

by affective phrasing of "When Sonny
Gets Blue" then final tune "Project S"
where Pepper's many notes all far less
than just one single by Harry Carney

Red's alto sound recalls Bird's at times
but never once his smooth melodic gift
Heath overheats as if from "thrift thrift
Horatio!" a rushing to wedding chimes

even K caught up with his *compañeros*
in urge to hurry but still he offers more
with pointed lines Cedar with tremolos
Reggie with him then solos Roy's four-

bar breaks he trades with full ensemble
on 2/25/66 Ken & Red will reassemble
for Blue Note broadcast on WABC-FM
with Cedar Ore & Walker fueling them

for "Jong Fu" flight where brass & reed
will meld together as if a fuselage takes
to the skies by an Alan Grant "Portraits
in Jazz" with KD & SR both in the lead

once Walton will chart their Sino route
& after the horns as one K then spread-
ing his wings the Chinese motif a hoot
cultural fun politically-incorrect ahead

swinging now over & beyond dynastic
walls no barrier to keep out aerial song
Red too flies by that same ching-chong
to a closed land opened with every lick

while Cedar working it into his piano's
bluesy chords supported by John Ore's
sturdy bass & then Hugh Walker solos
the rhythm too his drumming explores

on "Spring Is Here" Ken hewing to the-
matic line to find as if in marrow bones
its innermost nutritiousness or as in de-
posits deep in Earth the rich gemstones

Sonny probing too but with tonal touch
not so warm a sound metallic & intense
less affective than Cedar's no-nonsense
unflashy playing is solidly saying much

"Somewhere in the Night" features Son
alone then Grant requesting Ken to play
The Sandpiper theme '65 film with Tay-
lor painter Saint devoted wife to Burton

the Episcopal minister-headmaster lov-
ing delicious irreligious Liz two uncov-
ered by her former beau when Richard
stays with Eva Marie ending fitly hard

its theme "The Shadow of Your Smile"
Jack Sheldon with a nostalgic trumpet
turned into a vibratoed embellished hit
let the sadness of parting linger awhile

but K deconstructs the tune in a jaunty
take would maugre poor sound quality
locate its possibilities for dissecting of
memory's pleasure in pain-ridden love

& all such pieces more appealing than
Ken's "Straight Ahead" had cut before
for *Una más* & with Fathead Newman
would again in '67 that Texan on tenor

but still in '66 on July 4th to join the so-
called "missing link" Howard McGhee
following Gillespie influenced Navarro
& through him everyone from Brownie

on & perhaps Thad Jones third trumpet
for the Independence Day blowing get-
together of three brass with the rhythm
section of piano Billy Taylor the drum-

mer Albert Heath & brother Percy bass
each horn in turn playing "The Theme"
Miles motif K used at HARYOU space
& here he soloing first of trumpet team

a KD blend of melodic lines & double-
time runs & throws in as well a couple
of valvular trills his instrumental voice
can't confuse while somewhat at a loss

to know for certain but believe Maggie
McGhee's after the mellow Jones may-
be on fluegelhorn but least of the three
not quite at top of his game would say

Howard if it's he showing a "clipped"
Scott Yanow's word stop-&-go quirk-
iness of bebop's fillips or sudden blurt
its wit with which it ripped & quipped

on up-tempo "Blues" their trumpet trio
producing that brilliant & singular ring
of multiple brasses & each one soloing
all are gone & yet by sound none a zero

then K nothing till Blue Morocco date
of '67 he Sonny Cedar Paul Chambers
bass & drums a Hersh who remembers
still & all on April 16th privately taped

or was it on 10th at Minton's Playhouse
sources do not agree but "Bag's Groove"
opens their set soloists hot not to douse
but keep the flame alive as it's behoov-

ing of the jazz musician should ever do
yet regretful KD isn't on "What's New"
only Sonny solos after vocalist Joe Lee
renders its tender lyrics & their melody

but on Milt's perennial riff Ken follows
Red had repeated one phrase until it be-
came like a dog of neighbor will annoy
from howling same notes highs or lows

while K mixing running & single tones
none missing in swing as driving Cedar
picks up from him then as quickly owns
that Jackson groove his eight-to-the-bar

blocks built up on a kind of boogie base
till Paul with his always thoughtful bass
gets it said no tape static to take it away
as death did words poets "unable to say"

or "had been" in Strand's *Dark Harbor*
& then on the KD "Blue Bossa" theme
he & the altoist to do it more as a team
than even did with Henderson on tenor

K's solo on his original so wondrously
varied & maybe his best as he extends
a line swoops up down slow or speedy
then reiterates a phrase for telling ends

next after Sonny with Eric Dolphy-like
bursts of erratic notes make total sense
Cedar does his Horace Silver soul-type
version of this authentic nova of Ken's

on "I'll Remember April" after a vocal
Sonny solos & shows his mastery of ar-
peggiated chords but K makes of scalar
exercises runs more melodically logical

& on "Four" works through its changes
with his trademark ideational ease then
just can't get started in closer "Theme"
while Red receives ring of hydrangeas

& again on 8th of merry month of May
KD to hook up with Ronnie Matthews
piano & Paul on bass on drums Candy
Finch plus Fathead for a "Minor Blues"

slower Baby than planned but better so
with Ronnie setting the opening tempo
& later returns for some heavy search-
ing after David Newman comes on first

with his deliberate soulful tenor till KD
takes over & stays in the low & middle
range & on digging deep in his bag will
pull out a meditative mood consistently

on "Manhã de Carnaval" or also "Black
Orpheus" his nova approach newer rich-
er & simply lovely to this favorite of his
far finer by being live not a studio track

& Fathead into the spirit too as it seems
he is fully relating to the Bonfá theme's
bossa beat & Ronnie not dirty but down
Paul plucks fewer notes with conviction

in swinging Cole Porter's "I Love You"
K pausing after rapid runs to emphasize
nuanced tones or is it lost stamina bite's
going for a steer by its lip Pickett threw

tenor squeaking detracts from its other-
wise rip-roaring ride with rather touch-
ing turns & on flute later lends another
wind its time for moving equally much

piano bass & drums all pour it on most
on "Straight Ahead" almost overpower
KD's sound before the tenorist smokes
at such a furious pace can nearly cower

andante then for "Walkin'" a gait better
befits K's style than the frantic measure
yet suffers knock of uncontrollable sort
as tape breaks up to spoil half his effort

the glitch stopping when tenor comes in
with only a squawking reed now & then
subtracting from Fathead's strided stuff
Matthews again more than good enough

then Chambers slowing it all way down
reducing his notes to those choicest few
"walking" at the end as ever liked to do
taking care of business & going to town

to bring it full circle & right back home
to that theme Miles'd put on jazz's map
K & company closing set with a gloam-
ing before his recording one last '67 lap

on July 10th joins friend Cedar Walton
for his debut on *Cedar!* cut some dozen
years after serving his sideman duties in
others' bands as K has been & is hereon

yet free to experiment using novel mute
for "Turquoise Twice" starts the session
a motorcycle crash-helmet helps freshen
his sound & further add to its just repute

to Mark Gardner Ken's better each year
in the liner notes says his solo's a peach
in "Twilight Waltz" would seem to hear
his helmet's tone if ears don't overreach

together with piano gives a richer effect
to Cedar's slightly classical touch direct
& unpretentious but bouncy & witty on
"Short Stuff" & its "brief construction"

in Gardner's phrase while K's eccentric
twists & turns if new to amount to little
Vinnegar's bass & Higgins's drums kick
piano & trumpet along the "fiery fettle"

of Junior Cook only on opening & clos-
ing tunes the latter's the Duke's "Come
Sunday" its loud highs & then soft lows
a parallel to joy & prayer ending album

as Ken first & then the tenor worship in
almost sacred hush the Ellington service
to music & race a reverent K expression
of a religion of untranscendent Epicurus

& Cedar with long clean runs alternated
with warm left-hand chords consecrated
to the master of numinous song reoffers
the thanks are owed to all philosophers

"Take the 'A' Train" a bonus had deleted
from original disk with Kenny taking it
as a lower peak yet its climb completed
as if in preparation for *Trumpet Summit*

the '68 gauntlet challenge thrown down
in memory of & homage to Fats Brown-
ie & Booker Little died as said at just 23
in their honor 6 horns live at Club Ruby

with elder statesman K to show the way
leading off on "Bag's Groove" to begin
with sophistication & sense of direction
their Jamaica Queens tribute on 26 May

his smooth string of notes & then a high
pitch so perfect & sudden listener reacts
with a gasp of delight & yet K never try-
ing to impress but playing a line attracts

the deep-rooted ear his trill no frivolous
touch but a crux resolved before chorus
ends with a phrase aptly rounding it off
as a lecture delivered by a tenured prof

next Bill Hardman's grace notes galore
his lines less smooth than K's but even
so they have their point must believe in
an intent not execution & nothing more

then comes Ken's fellow Texan "Notes"
Williams of Galveston who with a hur-
ricane powerhouse style so dearly dotes
on gale winds blown in highest register

with "Confirmation" KD out of the gate
like a broncobuster hat in his hand keep-
ing time to a harmonic rodeo ride'll rate
him blue ribbon for sure top of the heap

now Hardman not so brash & with nice
theatrical asides & after a number splic-
ing between his lines that Parker theme
though now taking stagy to the extreme

& as for Richard (Williams' real name)
he's back with more to say fewer antics
at least at first but then repeats his same
up & unfollowed-through piercing licks

three other trumpets join Ken & Bill for
a five-man "Blues" plus rhythm section
with Woody Shaw replacing the similar
powerhousing of Notes in first selection

after Woody's screeches a Walter Kelly
adds hijinks to the other's pyrotechnics
before relief arrives at last as Ken picks
up his horn & syncopates o so soulfully

knows well if skill without any thought
it can't mean much as body best taught
by a guiding spirit & if up top to signify
it must be more than just reaching high

as even when Ken goes above the staff
every note's a part of his overall design
a serious link in his longer thinking line
witty may be but not to make one laugh

then Blue Mitchell true to his name fol-
lows suit with a mellow mood & before
the tape fades out Hardman with a hall-
mark mix of his technique & lineal lore

then "Sweet Clifford" closes the tribute
when Shaw again into his exhibitionism
wears down instead of uplifting her/him
Hardman amazing when gets to the root

with Williams hard to hear where if any-
where he's headed for & when Ken tries
to hear the chords can't with cacophony
of testosterone screams & outdoing cries

when such a memorial to early departed
had turned to noise & more competition
than a conference for honoring the men
did KD feel perhaps a little half-hearted

did he consider in his paying of respects
he had not resorted to show-boat effects
or regret had gone along with the crowd
straining in finale for sheer high & loud

whichever he must have known had out-
performed his younger rivals by remain-
ing himself in just another friendly bout
the only kind for which would ever train

Zodiacing

on 4th of June nine days after the Summit
Barry Harris' Sextet with KD on trumpet
records *Bull's Eye* the Motown leader-pi-
anist's "shooting match" that's musically

speaking the Gardner apropos liner notes
also say K's first record with Barry & his
friend Charles McPherson two associates
in Detroit when altoist then but now totes

a tenor on this session Schlitten produced
opening with Barry's title tune at extreme
up-tempo yet never too fast for a spruced-
up K's rarin' to sight their targeted theme

lets fly first with his "superb articulation"
his speed & flow would've knocked Bird
out on remembering him from days when
he & Ken drovered together heading herd

Charles even compared with other Chazz
when he'd played on occasion a tenor too
as McPherson here & deserves such a ku-
do for that horn handled so well as he has

on baritone Pepper Adams can rarely con-
vince in terms of sound or sense but adds
a depth to ensemble's tone & PA has won
a pat on the back in Mark's liners ee-gads

then Barry recalls Bud Powell's phrasing
& chords in a sizzling chorus but's better
timeless could say on "Clockwise" where
it's just a trio with Higgins all're praising

& Chambers soloing arco is laudable too
while the pianist on "Off Monk" his bou-
quet paid to that prophet himself imitates
the rhythmic & tonal ways he deliberates

only Pepper's squeak to mar the homage
though made up for by K & tenor's com-
plementary play with trumpeter's engag-
ing lines relaxed but virile top to bottom

& McPherson reminding how the Mobe
could fit with Ken hand-in-glove & now
the tenorist swinging on a similar bough
another pea in a pod or the pinna to lobe

on Barry's "Barengo" a "sinuous tango"
jazzed up by bary's anchor as KD leads
this piece is after his heart with its lingo
knows from S.A. tour had planted seeds

clear from his later solo so relaxed once
more & yet all over his horn as he hunts
for & finds the Latin pulse he had heard
firsthand its New World he'd discovered

yet a land well known too by tenor man
who's conversant in its native speech as
even Pepper whose baritone's more fas-
cinating with its slower "scorching" can

also be & Harris's piano with an almost
Kenton kind of "Peanut Vendor" riposte
& next a fine trio version of "Off Minor"
classic they render in Thelonious' honor

then sextet concludes with "O So Basal"
shows again why so many had invited K
to participate in recording sessions as all
knew could depend on him in every way

to lead or follow contribute a solo or sup-
port another's & never selfish no fanatic
of a single style neither manic nor erratic
& with talents to spare not ever puffed up

his chorus a super display of every tech-
nique in his bag of tidbits his gift for sur-
prise & delight with nothing for the heck
of it a "pregnant pause" then even juicier

with tenor bary & piano all too offering
breaks "trenchant" or "spiky and mean"
a "hip" quote before Billy's drums bring
it home the last note Ken's long & clean

at the end of July on the 30th to be exact
KD to appear at NYC's Top of the Gate
with pianist Toshiko Akiyoshi a live act
of both + reed bass & drums still in '68

the first piece her own "Opus No. Zero"
nothing of Japan but of a "stop-and-go"
Blakey Messengers' "hard bop rhythm"
as right on it Ken Dryden set his thumb

while K's himself as he carries the load
& states theme with a lift strong as ever
flexing his chorus as anytime he soloed
in chase takes on Lew Tabackin's tenor

& in playing "How Insensitive" straight
with Lew on flute after the piano embel-
lishes Jobim tune they like waves swell-
ing subsiding rise fall intensify or abate

for "The First Night" K more meditative
following the piano & flute in a classical
vein & before his-Lew-drum's explosive
notes break up a spell properly nocturnal

soloing on "Phrygian Waterfall" Toshiko
keeps modal flow by a left-hand ostinato
but on her "gospel-drenched" "Let's Roll
in Sake" into Nat-Cannonball kinda soul

with a demanding part for Ken but never
anything to sweat for cut KD ever would
any given him no solo here she'll feature
him on their next tune as well she should

since K made "Morning of the Carnival"
almost his own not Bonfá's song a piece
he'd recorded at home & abroad & as al-
ways his flutter-tongue to lend new lease

on the listener's life & with his sixteenth
notes on Tosh's "My Elegy" his strength
& total control still intact his chorus fast
as any he played to play long as he'd last

Brownie lost to accident Lee to homicide
Booker to a kidney disease awaiting Ken
& on previous April 4th the assassination
of Dr. King in decade the Kennedys died

Martin's eclipse under the astrology sign
of Aries the ram whose image on *Zodiac*
Donna Jordan drew first in order to align
her sleeve-art figures with monthly track

of the dozen constellations & second be-
cause 12/16/68 album begins with Cecil
Payne's in memoriam MLK on bass Wil-
bur Ware Al Heath drums Wynton Kelly

piano with Cecil on both baritone & alto
as KD pays tribute with his opening solo
to the man who had his mountain dream
in Duke song lyrics none to tear its seam

not in Nashville not anywhere even if he
kept like Moses from that promised land
got locked up in Birmingham jail to free
at last those of a color Jim Crow banned

at times K's burred tone & slight vibrato
sob for & shudder from loss his notes on
coming down tremble a keen high to low
at others his lines lament & yet all blown

with his jubilating flow in celebration of
a life elected though aware it would lead
to a James Earl Ray out of belief in need
for non-violence justice & Christian love

Payne on bary carries on his own mourn-
ing for that peaceful protest marcher torn
apart by the high-powered NRA's sacred
Second's right to bear klan-armed hatred

Cecil's gruff low tones with Kelly's elec-
tric piano underscoring grief of Thoreau-
Gandhi disciples at fall of another heroic
follower yet comforted by where he'd go

far for sure from "Girl, you got a home"
& yet this second Cecil tune moving too
although in another way as he & Ken to-
gether besting K with any other baritone

their sound unmatched by either Adams-
K or Davis-K & in soloing Payne terrific
from beginning to end neither bim-bams
thank you mam nor quick flim-flam trick

& then a relaxed KD with superior swing
& more so again after a "pregnant pause"
as Kelly's chords contribute to the cause
for his unrushed blue notes keep it going

"Slide Hampton" a letdown where Ken's
concerned his brief break's not up to par
but up to speed is Payne both his engines
firing first on bary then alto bar-after-bar

on "Follow Me" another Cecil up-tempo
his bary solo more daring still as now he
just lets go & how K takes in after him o
me o my with turns of phrases o so witty

& once Ware & Heath have traded fours
Al sets off alone to do his drummer thing
before the final piece the leader's "Flying
Fish" with pectoral fins for wings it soars

as does this Payne quintet on rumba beat
or some dance done in a Caribbean street
Cecil's bary solo lifted out of tropics' sea
& into flight by Wynton Wilbur & Tootie

& the pianist's own chorus so plenty fine
& to end the session K too brings his real
feel for this Afro-Latin rhythm Al cosign-
ing his notes with subtly crashing cymbal

& then in spring of '69 Ken with thirteen-
year-old Donna's dad on Clifford's "new
phase" Dolphy series recording of "872"
recalls that year's tragic tumultous scene

of another Tet attack & a Black Panther
militant stand shooting of Huey Cleaver
in exile Hilliard too Seale Hoover F.B.I.
& near the end Hampton & Clark to die

but Ken just part of ensemble sound not
taking any in yo face nor any angry solo
never one to complain still wonder what
he thought of radicals racist pigs & Mao

did he side in his mind more with a King
or a Carmichael with Black empowering
or reject imperiling his teeth as Satchmo
said he'd be no good if he couldn't blow

on his tenor Jordan now up to date on all
the enraged & raw-toned raucous school
ousts bop & fist-pumps death to the cool
but in his notes hear less hate than usual

& on Cliff's "Quagoudougou" the lower
tones on his horn his trill a sudden honk
& picked-off high-up pitch deliver more
of beauty than any urge to bonk or conk

then KD works out his own "new phase"
yet after two kinds of bop no other craze
came natural to him though still to show
he could do it too & was willing to grow

his solo even so doesn't swing not up to
his older routine & Julian Priester trom-
bone break nothing great while Wynton
with his groovy rock fits into old or new

two drummers Ed & Roy rambunctious
but tenor's best here on his *In the World*
whose trend Ken inhabited in living just
this once soon eviction from that of Bird

for after one performance in August '70
when his chops Yanow says failing him
in playing at Roosevelt College in mem-
ory of CP on his birth's 50th anniversary

KD never recorded again his own sound
on this earth never made by any trumpet
even if any better players to come found
his horn or its brand could never make it

& even though he pauses more the spark
still there & will on "Summertime" hark
back to the old fire of those earlier years
with legends Yard 'Trane & all his peers

but first "Just Friends" with his scintillat-
ing runs & that burnished tone can never
mistake for another's can never overrate
its warmth his always getting it together

& then Ken introduces in his tenor voice
to be taped no more for the listener alive
the Gershwin as Ray Nance's violin jive
opens its bluesiness for which all rejoice

if KD's stamina's beginning to fade still
to hear him every trumpeter has to envy
such sustained power the unbowed will
to honor his mentor by undying melody

remembering through every trill & tone
a note shaken up high held long or short
all the Bird solos he had gotten by heart
before arriving in NYC nearly unknown

but making a mark as his star would rise
not in a CP sky with gazers all so idolize
nor ever to inspire scrawls of "KD lives"
& yet his musical gift still gives & gives

Expiring

all the breaths once taken in & then let
out for words sung notes from trumpet
exhaled tongued staccato emitted long
for a sharp flat accidental natural song

the airflow divided up in bars of duple
triple quadruple time the tones to vary
in length & mood observing as a pupil
signatures for meter & to read the key

a life's continuum early middle & late
though still four years from fifty when
had to take work as a music-store ven-
dor & postal clerk with no record date

his cabaret card had lost & on dialysis
union dues unpaid membership expir-
ing meant no blood transfusion all this
while the girls grew up with NYU hir-

ing him as part-time bringing in some
& liked teaching but its pay minimum
had been to Austin for their Longhorn
Jazz Festival April 28-30 '67 perform-

ing with the Sam Houston State Band
& to write for June's *Down Beat* issue
his report on event with its who's who
from Monk Diz & Blakey to outstand-

ing fellow Texans Arnett Cobb Clean-
head Vinson Jimmy Ford Buddy Tate
Cedric Haywood & Charles Patterson
Teddy Wilson native hometown great

Ernie & Emilio Cáceres Larry Coryell
the Bayou City-raised Illinois Jacquet
plus drum legend Jo & the modern El-
vin unkin Joneses together for one set

wrote of Jo had played "with the ease
and grace that kings are made of" Art
"*fuerte y con mucho fuego*" & on the part
of the young "White Power" 21-piece

"supporting cast" said for it & K boss
arrangements that audience screamed
his "what else?" shows never at a loss
for drollery as language too esteemed

hoped to play or even to write his way
to Diz's tremendous level & for '70 K
to produce indeed his so fine too-brief
memoir Fragment a modest self-belief

the next year or the one after to phone
university in Austin saying might relo-
cate he'd enjoy playing in its jazz-pro-
gram band & helping students to hone

their skills had plans for setting up his
treatments there D Goodwin directing
the ensemble then & remembered this
& having arranged before K's passing

his "Epitaph" & performing the chart
at Chicago's national college jazz fes-
tival in '72 December 5th K breathless
from renal failure had stopped a heart

a brain filled with unseen notes heard
within his inner ears then out of tubes
& a gold or silver bell the valve lubes
had speeded along Messengers' word

a prophetic phrase blues or bossa beat
a chase or a smoky-toned running line
to blend with any instrument compete
with none but under the brothers' sign

Cecil Payne recalling at his Brooklyn
family-man home K taught him a roll
& toodle on baritone looked sick skin
color *very* dry last seen at jazz mobile

studio where all there but Kenny grip-
ing about a musician's economic state
he quiet just holding his horn no hype
with him had accepted his chosen fate

had carried him to Scandinavia Brazil
& Paree Post Oak to Frisco & to NYC
learning lyrics & through them to feel
& to the recorded sounds he'll ever be

About the Author

Dave Oliphant is a native Texan poet, a recently retired (2006) senior lecturer at the University of Texas in Austin, the editor of *The Library Chronicle,* a noted writer on the history of Jazz in Texas, and editor/publisher of Prickly Pear Press. His recent books include a volume of poems, *Backtracking* (2004), a collection of essays, *Jazz Mavericks of the Lone Star State* (2007), and two translations of collections of Chilean poetry: *Love Hound* by Oliver Welden (winner of the poetry prize at the 2007 New York Book Festival) and *After Dinner Declarations* by Nicanor Parra (2009). Oliphant's 548-page memoir, *Harbingers of Books to Come: A Texan's Literary Life,* was published by Wings Press in 2009.

Oliphant was born in Fort Worth in 1939. He graduated from the University of Texas with an M.A. and took his Ph.D. at Northern Illinois University. Dave and his wife María, a native of Chile, have been married for 45 years and have a son and a daughter and four grandchildren.

Colophon

This first edition of *KD: A Jazz Biography*, by Dave Oliphant, has been printed on 70 pound non-acidic Arbor paper by Edwards Brothers of Ann Arbor, Michigan. Titles have been set in Bernhard Modern type, the text in Adobe Caslon type. All Wings Press books are designed and produced by Bryce Milligan.

On-line catalogue and ordering:
www.wingspress.com

Wings Press titles are distributed
to the trade by the
Independent Publishers Group
www.ipgbook.com
and in Europe by
www.gazellebookservices.co.uk

Also available as an ebook.